T0148017

CROSSING THE LINE

MEMOIRS OF A FAIRFAX COUNTY POLICE OFFICER

CONSTANCE CURRAN NOVAK

IUNIVERSE, INC.
NEW YORK   BLOOMINGTON

Crossing the Line
Memoirs of a Fairfax County Police Officer

iUniverse books may be ordered through booksellers or by contacting:

iUniverse
1663 Liberty Drive
Bloomington, IN 47403
www.iuniverse.com
1-800-Authors (1-800-288-4677)

Because of the dynamic nature of the Internet, any Web addresses or links contained in this book may have changed since publication and may no longer be valid.

ISBN: 978-1-4502-1328-8 (sc)
ISBN: 978-1-4502-1329-5 (dj)
ISBN: 978-1-4502-1741-5 (ebk)

Printed in the United States of America

iUniverse rev. date: 3/15/2010

This book is dedicated to the men and women around the world who have devoted their lives to improving life through law enforcement, to my children Ronnie and Crystal who were forced to grow up and make sacrifices in a home where both parents were cops, and to my sister Sharon, whose support made this dream a reality.

CONTENTS

PREFACE

Fairfax County sits just outside Washington DC in northern Virginia. Once a rural playground, Fairfax has become a bustling metropolis of Fortune 500 firms, corporate headquarters, information technology businesses, trade associations, and foreign-owned companies and is also home to the CIA (Central Intelligence Agency) and countless businessmen, congressmen, senators, and state, local, and national heads of government. Fairfax County residents enjoy one of the highest median family incomes in the country, as well as one of the best public school systems, and, of course, one of the finest and most prestigious law enforcement agencies. With more than one million residents and 399 squares miles, Fairfax County has seen tremendous growth. The demand for services and the response to such demands has turned Fairfax County into one of the most sought-after communities in which to live and work.

The Fairfax County Police Department was established in 1940 in the basement of an office building with only five officers performing the duties of law enforcement. Almost seventy years later, the police department has increased to more than thirteen hundred sworn officers who occupy ten major facilities and several other smaller sites. The number of female police officers has not grown very much over the years. In 1979, there were about twenty-five female officers, and today, there are only about 182. The police department has relied on superior training and selection of employees with the highest moral and ethical standards to become the nationally respected agency that it is today. The stories contained here are real. They are but a few of the experiences that I lived through. The names that are mentioned herein are fictitious. My goal in writing this book was to express myself in such a way that everyone can understand the life of a police officer and have new insight and respect for the law enforcement family. Of course, my perspective is from a woman's point of view, but up until now, few people knew anything about the life of a woman police officer.

1

PLANTING THE SEED

My earliest childhood memories include the excitement of reading whodunit books and playing the game of CLUE. I was intrigued with the idea of taking clues and trying to figure out who the bad guy was. My favorite books were Alfred Hitchcock murder mysteries. I bought one of the original hard cover books at a garage sale a few years ago for fifty cents, and it now sits proudly up on the shelf with all my college and police books. So it probably came as no surprise to the family that I would become involved in law in one fashion or another. But at five feet two inches and ninety-nine pounds, not too many people expected me to become a police officer, especially in 1979 when the police force of seven hundred in Fairfax County had only twenty-six women.

I was primarily raised by a mother who believed that people could do anything they wanted as long as they had the desire. She proved that in many ways. My mother raised four children following the end of World War II while having a full-time career and pursuing other personal interests. She was the drummer in a band, a singer, a writer, and a role model for my future pursuits. When all four kids were out in the world on their own, Mom decided to see what the world could offer her. The beauty of brickwork caught her attention. She considered it to be creative work, and she enjoyed working with her hands. After two or three classes, she found she wasn't built to be a bricklayer, and at five feet four inches, 120 pounds, the strength of hauling wheelbarrow loads of bricks around wasn't in her. But she had the guts to try and go after something different. I was taught that there wasn't anything I couldn't do.

I graduated from George Mason University in 1979 with a bachelor's degree in law enforcement. I knew when I entered college that I wanted to do something in law, but I wasn't sure what. When I started taking law enforcement classes in my second year, I decided to be a police officer. While still in college, I began the tedious interviewing and testing process to become a police officer. Because of my size, I knew the most difficult part was going to be the physical demands, so I tried to prepare myself by running and lifting weights. I found out that one part of the test required that I push a car with a man in it about twenty feet. A friend of mine, Tim, had a Trans AM, which weighed about the same as a police cruiser. We drove down to a nearby shopping center to practice. Tim showed me how to use my legs to push rather than my back and upper body, and I was able to push the car and the driver the required distance without much difficulty. All that changed the day of the test.

There were six of us taking the physical agility test, which included running, performing sit- ups and push-ups, pulling ourselves through a window, and scaling a ladder to the top of a three-story building. Everything went well until it came time to push the car, but after practicing with Tim's car, I was confident that I would be successful. The instructor got behind the wheel of the car and told us we would have two chances in which to push the car the required distance. I got a little nervous when a male went before me and took both tries to successfully push the car. When my name was called, I positioned myself to the rear of the car, placed my back up against the bumper, and pushed with my legs. The car moved about four feet and stopped. I asked the instructor if the brake was on, and he replied no. I sat back down and watched the others attempt the car push and fought back tears as hopes of becoming a police officer slowly faded.

As I watched the others struggle, I noticed that the instructor was putting on the brake right at the beginning to prevent the car from rolling backward. I pointed this out and asked the instructor if he could please move the car to another area of the parking lot because I didn't think that it was on perfectly level ground. The instructor looked at me for what seemed like an eternity before he agreed to move the car, but I would still only have one more chance to push it. I wasn't the only one in the same predicament. Two others had failed to push the car the first time, and one of them was a man nearly twice my size. When my turn came up, I took a deep breath and somehow turned inside to find just a little extra strength. After carefully positioning myself, I began to push the four thousand-pound automobile. When I got to the twenty-foot mark, I was so happy that I felt like I had just finished the Boston Marathon. Not all six of us made it that day. But I knew that this was my new beginning.

There were many more grueling interviews and physical tests in the weeks to follow. Although the testing process usually takes months, they rushed me through because an academy class was beginning soon. I endured a lengthy interview to determine why I wanted to be a police officer and what my goals were, as well as a battery of psychological tests, a polygraph test, and more physical agility tests.

Finally, I was hired to begin the Fairfax County Criminal Justice Academy. I was never so excited about anything in my life. I didn't even know what the job paid or what the benefits were. I soon realized that for a single person, the salary wasn't bad, but if I ever hoped to raise a family, I should have a backup plan.

In 1979, the police academy was sixteen weeks long (it is now twenty-two weeks). It was much like I imagined boot camp, only the hours were better. Experienced officers prepared us for the unexpected and taught us how to apply the laws, defend ourselves, shoot straight, and drive at high speeds.

When learning defensive tactics, we boxed to learn how to block a blow and how to effectively strike another person. I was paired up with a recruit who had boxing experience so the instructor thought he could control his punches. We had sparred for a few minutes when he clobbered me in the mouth with a right hook. My response was a punch to his solar plexus that took his breath away. I felt my lip swell, but I realized I was capable of incapacitating an attacker if it were ever necessary. I had never needed to defend myself before, so getting punched in the face for the first time was a real eye opener.

In the academy we had to learn to shoot with a handgun and a shotgun. My dad taught me to shoot light bulbs with a .22 when I was ten years old, so my shooting abilities were good. I listened well to my instructors and shot "expert" every time. I got knocked over the first day when I fired the shotgun, but I had full respect for its power after that. My nickname in the academy was "Little Feet," which I received after the range instructor asked me how my little feet could hold me up. It stuck for a long time.

Running was also a big part of the police academy. Two miles a day was tough for me. I am not built to run; with my short legs, I felt like I was running twice as much as everyone else. But I would stay late some days and get tips from the physical training instructor. I would often cramp up when I ran, and the instructor told me to push in on the area of the cramp, and it would go away. This usually worked, but not on the day of the final PT exam. I ran the first mile okay, and then this sharp pain came into my side. I pushed in on it and kept running until the pain became almost unbearable. Everyone else was passing me, and I could see the finish line up ahead about a quarter mile. I feared that I wouldn't make the time limit. My PT instructor ran up alongside me asking what was wrong. I told him about the pain that wouldn't go away. He told me that if I were able to keep the pace I was running, I would still make the maximum allotted time. I kept running even though I felt like my insides were burning up. As I approached the finish line, the last to come in, my whole academy class was cheering me on. I took the final step and collapsed. I was taken to the hospital and diagnosed with an inflamed appendix. But I had made it.

I remember the day I came home and showed my mom my new uniform, which had to be tailor-made. I had everything polished and was looking good until I had to put on the bulletproof vest. I am a woman who hates bras anyway, so wearing a bulletproof vest ten to twelve hours a day equates me to the man in the iron mask. I'd compare it to an 1800s era corset, but those were designed to make a woman look prettier and her figure more flattering. A bulletproof vest is designed to save your life by slowing the impact of bullets. The weight of it flattens your figure to an almost concave design. To take it off each night was like taking a size ten foot out of a size eight shoe. My own mother laughed when she first saw it. They tried to give it "cups" so that it was more comfortable to wear, but it ended up making me look like Dolly Parton. I took it back to the manufacturer and told them to take about five layers out of the cups. They told me it would not offer the same protection, but at this point, I didn't care.

There were also other aspects of the uniform that were a burden. I had to buy boys' T-shirts and boys' black socks. The only thing feminine on me was my panties. Having a size five foot didn't help either. I looked everywhere for shoes to fit; no one had them. I finally had to buy combat boots in a boy's size that had the word junior written in them. (Only my closest friends ever knew that.) My hips took a pounding from the gun belt. I had bruises on both hips a lot and frequently had lower back pain, but when you're in a male-dominated occupation, you have to adapt.

There were other minor arduous elements of the job that made life more difficult for women recruits, like the fact that the cruisers had bench seats that wouldn't go up far enough. And because there were so few women on the police force, my locker was in the men's locker room. I would go into the bathroom for the personal stuff like putting on an undershirt and slacks and then put on the bullet proof vest and polish my shoes and brass in the locker room. The men didn't seem to mind too much, and I just looked down a lot.

2

"I WANT A MAN!"

There are lots of reasons that police work is especially hard on women. We have the macho cops that feel we are invading their manhood, and we have the old-timers that feel we should be barefoot and pregnant. It is difficult to date as a female cop and even more difficult to marry and have children; most people don't picture a mother going out on a midnight shift, chasing bad guys, and locking up drunks. The uniform does not conform to the shape of a woman, and it's heavy to boot. I weighed about thirteen more pounds with my vest, gun belt, and boots on than I did before I got dressed. And I was only ninety-nine pounds to begin with. My hips were often sore and bruised, and my lower back was achy. I had to lean on my handcuffs because my waist was too small to pull them around to the side—if they had added one more thing to the gun belt, I would have had to strap it to my leg.

I don't do anything different because I am a woman, either. I still change my own flat tires and those of disabled motorists. I still have to sit in on classes involving sexual deviants and try not to show how disgusted and grossed out I am. I still have to crank up that chain saw when a tree falls across my path in a storm. I still have to stand in the freezing rain directing traffic around a fatal accident. And I still have to spend fifteen minutes more than the guys getting dressed after shift to try and transform myself back into a girl. I'm not complaining, but don't have me come to your door to take some silly theft report and say, "I want a man!"

I drove up to this beat-up old house with a beat-up old woman standing out front. I introduced myself and asked her how I could help. She looked at me and said, "I want a man." "Okay," I responded, "but is there something I can do for you?" She said, "No. I called the police, and I want a man!"

It had been a long night, and I felt like wishing her luck and walking away, but I knew that probably wasn't a good idea. After much more battering, I contacted my supervisor, a man, and he responded. I thought he would take the report himself but was pleasantly surprised to hear him say, "This officer is perfectly capable of handling any problem you may have, and you can either talk to her, or we will be on our way." Yes! Two points for the female cop, no points for the demented old hag. The woman reluctantly let me in to talk with her, and I reluctantly wrote a report, but I was angry that she didn't think I was good enough to handle her problem.

DO WHAT IT TAKES AND THEN DO A LITTLE MORE

I served as a police diver for five years. It was a voluntary role that we did along with our other police responsibilities, but I loved to dive, so why not do it at work? Our outfit was called the Underwater Search and Recovery Team, which was a freestanding unit of volunteers. We didn't go after the man who just fell through the ice; we went after the man who fell through the ice ten hours ago. We weren't rescue; we were recovery. There was something very eerie about feeling my way around a pond with absolutely no visibility, looking for a body. In one respect, I hoped I wouldn't find it. In another, I hoped I did, so I could get out and bring closure to the family. There is nothing quite like the sensation of touching a frozen dead body before even seeing it. It is like a horror flick.

We don't have any clear ponds or rivers in Fairfax County—the water is black or green, and we must feel for everything we are looking for. I have dived for bodies, weapons, stolen property, and cars and didn't get paid any extra for it. But I liked doing a lot of different things, and it gave me a good feeling when we either found something or eliminated an area as a source for evidence. In one such pond that was a runoff for a concrete company, we dove for a stolen car. The water had a bright green tint to it and a chemical smell. By the time we found the car, brought it up, and got out of the water, our skin burned. We had to be treated for skin irritations for several days.

One frozen January night, a seventeen-year-old boy decided to swing out over the Lorton rock quarry with a can of spray paint to draw his name on the rocks. He had taken an old rope from his father's shed, not knowing it had dry rot. His friends watched in horror as the rope snapped, causing him to plummet some sixty feet, hitting several rocks on his way down. Rescue workers found no one on the surface of the water, so the dive team began recovery efforts the next morning.

It took longer to suit up than it took to find the body, because he had been wearing a heavy coat and mountain climbing boots. When he fell into the icy waters, he sank quickly and stayed near the rock wall. Within ten minutes we touched what felt like a leg and clothing in about fifteen feet of water and pulled him to the surface. Family members and media watched closely as we loaded him into a body bag.

I left the team after five years. It seemed that a promotion I had received within the police department threatened a subordinate officer who was a more experienced diver. He wanted me off the team because I outranked him, and because of that, I should be calling the shots. But he had more diving experience and may have been better at articulating reasons for doing things a certain way. I understood his thinking and would have agreed that the more experienced diver should supervise—had he not been the one who removed a piece of evidence at the scene of my underwater test so I couldn't find it. The test was required to become a member of the dive team—even though we were all cops and all certified divers, most of us had no experience in recovering property or bodies, so they tested us on compass courses as well as rope courses.

Part of the testing process was to find certain items in zero-visibility water in a certain amount of time. The last object was a hammer, and I couldn't find it anywhere. I was later told that this same officer took it out of the water so I would not pass the test. Other than a stern talking to, he was never disciplined for his actions. I made the team despite him. I was certified in deep diving, ice diving, search and rescue, and scuba lifesaving and accident management

(SLAM), as well as underwater photography, but this wasn't enough for him.

The subordinate went to his major to complain that there were too many "chiefs" on the team and not enough "Indians." Now this particular major was the same one who had made his wife quit the police force and had been overheard leaving a command staff meeting saying, "There are 9 percent women on this department, and that is 9 percent too many." So I was not surprised when I was removed from the team. I fought it and made a formal complaint about it, which led to the major's somewhat sudden retirement. I was asked by the human resources supervisor what it would take to get me to drop the complaint. All I wanted was recognition for my abilities and formal documentation that the subordinate officer had tried to hamper my efforts to be a part of the team. With that done, I resigned from the team.

I never believed in trying to get out of something because I was a woman or trying to gain something for the same reason. I worked hard at my job and wanted to be treated equally. No more, no less. I hated hearing about a woman who sued a police department because she couldn't qualify with the shotgun by stating she shouldn't have to carry one. Or the woman who felt she should get special treatment because she had kids and needed to work strictly day work. I would always go to the other extreme and go out on a limb to prove myself. I was the one who was actually knocked over the first time I shot a shotgun because I didn't know what the recoil was like, and I went down on two knees instead of one to fire it. The recoil knocked me on my back. The instructors saw it coming but chose not to say anything in advance so I would learn for myself. I learned all right. I then took other classes to become more confident with the weapons and soon after became a firearms instructor. I was also the only woman ever to compete in the interdepartmental pistol team competitions. I took home a third place trophy one day, which sits proudly on my shelf of police paraphernalia.

When I was on the dive team, we had to take an ice diving course. I was the only one who had to take the course in a wet suit instead of a dry suit because they didn't have any small enough to fit me. The test for the class was to drill a hole in the ice, extend a line from it to another hole in the ice, and swim the length. I was under the ice for about fifteen minutes in a wet suit, while the others stayed dry and comfortable in their dry suits. I had a severe headache for a week but never complained, because I wanted the position and didn't want any exceptions made because I was a woman. I always knew I had to do a little more. I was the one who volunteered for all the special assignments and agreed to be attacked by the K-9 dog when the team came to our station to put on a demonstration. I was the one who drove the paddy wagon because no one else wanted to.

Sometimes citizens would ride with police officers to gain a better knowledge of what police officers do. I was the one who took the ride-along (or Satan, as I preferred to call him) so no one else would have to. This was the kid who wanted to be a police officer but never would because of his mental aptitude. He would do chores around the station in exchange for an occasional ride-along. The night I had him, he didn't speak a word for forty-five minutes until he threw up in my cruiser. I took him back to the station and made him hose out my car. He told the sergeant I made him nervous. That was his farewell ride-along.

Another task I took on was to learn to operate a chain saw. After a week of severe storms one spring, all the stations received chain saws so that we would be equipped to cut down trees that had fallen across the roadways. A class was offered to qualify people to use the chain saws. Once again, I was the only woman. I didn't have a burning desire to be qualified in chain saw operation, but I did want to show others that I was not a small, blonde, female supervisor that made it as far as she did because of her gender. I wanted to be known as the small, blonde supervisor that wasn't afraid of anything and made it as far as I did despite my gender. I knew I would have to constantly prove myself, but I also thought that after fifteen or twenty years on the job, the guys would start to let up. That never happened.

A Woman in a Man's Land

I didn't really feel awkward being the only woman on my squad and only one of four women at my station, because I was so focused on the job itself. My field training officer was a man about six feet three inches, who had to wedge his knees up against the glove box when I drove because I needed to pull the cruiser's bench seat all the way up in order to use the pedals. He never complained. I expected to have problems with the older officers who had been around a long time and probably thought women belonged in the kitchen. What I got was exactly the opposite.

The older male officers would look at me with wrinkled brows and big question marks in their eyes. They watched my every move, never saying a word. One older officer in particular, John, was my backup one night and asked me to meet him at a nearby shopping center when our call was over. When I pulled up next to his cruiser, I expected him to tell me to find another job. But to my surprise, he told me he had serious doubts when he first saw me but decided to sit back and just watch for a while. He told me that I was all right. Then he gave me a little smile and shook his head and drove off into the night. I'll never forget him.

Another older officer named Lou, who had a reputation for checking out all the garage sales on Saturday mornings, was a real hoot to work with. He seldom had anything nice to say to anyone, and he was always off by himself. His wife packed him a lunch every day, and he did as little work as he could get by with. If he was ever given a case at the end of a shift, we could hear his voice in complaint all over the station. I really don't know why people like that go into law enforcement, but I guess he felt he had invested so much time in the job that it wasn't worth looking for something else. Like everyone else, I just stayed away from him. But one day I backed him up on a burglar alarm. He never felt he needed backup, but I went anyway. Of course, he didn't wait for me to arrive, opting to go in and check out everything by himself.

I had never seen him draw his weapon until that day. When I pulled up, he came out of the house with eyes the size of silver dollars. He said that he heard voices inside. As we entered the house, all I could hear was the deafening sound of the alarm. We checked out the first floor of the large, well furnished house and announced ourselves in case some innocent party was at home. No one was there. When we got to the top floor, I, too, heard voices. I couldn't make out what was being said because of the alarm, but it was definitely more than one person.

With guns drawn, we slowly and methodically made our way down the hall to the last room to be checked. We shoved open the door, and drew down on ... two very talkative parrots that were probably as scared as we were. Lou was never the same after that. He told that story to everyone. I don't think he ever denied backup again, and the job seemed more fun to him after that.

Some of the younger officers felt that my presence threatened their machismo. Some of them made my life very difficult, even making up lies to try and make me look bad. I vividly remember one such occasion. I was a master police officer, which is a senior patrol officer rank. I had about five years on the force at the time. One night I was assigned the field, which meant I could go anywhere in my district. Two other officers were told there was a carnival in their area and to check on it from time to time. At one point I heard the officers tell the dispatcher that they were out with two subjects at the far end of the shopping center. The officers were running criminal checks on them, which told me there might be a problem, so I started down there to back them up. When I arrived, the officers were casually talking with the two men because the warrant officer was backed up, and it was taking quite awhile to return any information about whether the two men were wanted. The officers had been on foot, so I stuck around in case they needed a transport back to their cruisers or one of the men was wanted and needed to be transported.

It was a steamy August night, and I had my arm out the window with the air conditioning on. One of the men came up to my car and asked me what the master police officer patch on my sleeve meant. I told him it was just a ranking structure in the police department. He then asked me why I was in an air-conditioned cruiser and the other two guys were out on foot in the heat of the night. Jokingly, I said, "Because I am smarter than they are." The two officers later went back to the station and twisted the story around to say that I told a man that the master police officer symbol on my sleeve meant that I was smarter than the other officers. I was very upset not only because it made me look bad with the troops but also because the two officers knew this was a lie and were just mad at the fact that I was of higher rank than they were. They purposely made me out to look bad. I confronted them and got a weak, "Oh, I must not have heard it right." But the damage was done.

Back in the early 80s, officers were promoted because they did well on a test and interview and proved themselves worthy of a promotion. That is the way it should be, but some officers didn't like the fact that I received a promotion before them. The way I looked at it, that was their problem, and I would continue to do my job as expected and with much enthusiasm. Those that felt threatened would either have to accept it and move on or go work for someone else.

I found out after about six months on the job that there was a bet going around as to who would get me in bed first. They all lost. I expected this kind of thing, so I wasn't too surprised. I was there for one thing and one thing only. As a result, my work spoke for itself, and I was promoted to higher ranks. Once I got to sergeant and then second lieutenant, I was able to make changes by showing the men I had the road experience necessary to supervise a squad. I finally gained the respect that had been so difficult to obtain early on.

DON'T BUST MY BUBBLE

Two things people assume about cops: they don't get arrested, and they don't lie. Boy was my bubble burst. An officer called me early one morning from the academy where he was taking an in-service class and told me that an officer had walked into his class and told everyone that a twenty-year veteran who we all knew had been arrested for bank robbery. Everyone was in complete shock. Many thought it was a joke. Everyone's reaction was the same: "Him? No way." This officer was very quiet—by no means a go-getter but not one who complained all the time or thought "he was owed." He was arrested for about six bank robberies in three different jurisdictions. The ones he committed in our county were done during a meal break from the job, while he was on duty. To this day, no one knows why he did it. His own wife, who was a dispatcher for us, didn't know. He told a fellow officer that he would let everyone know why when all the court cases were over. I was told that he married a younger woman after he divorced his first wife, and he just wanted to keep her in the lifestyle that the two had grown accustomed to. Years later, I was talking with another officer about this case, and he told me that he had been on a stakeout for the bank robber with the officer who was the one actually robbing the banks!

That was the most shocking case. Every now and then you'll hear of a bad cop getting involved in drugs or some other such case, but those are rare. Still more painful is the cop that lies to protect himself at the cost of another officer's career. Unfortunately, I was at the losing end of one of those. The details are not important. I had been on the department for about sixteen years. The event wasn't even a major one, but for four months I was under the lights of Internal Affairs, having been brought up on charges of performance of duty and truthfulness. The truthfulness charge alone would have gotten me fired. Everyone involved was under a gag order. No one could talk about the incident, so I couldn't tell anyone my side of the story. I was looked at by everyone as "the liar."

People I had been friends with (or so I thought) stopped talking to me. I feared for my job.

Internal Affairs talks to the accused person last. Finally, after four months of anguish, I was called to Internal Affairs and questioned for two hours. It wasn't until that day that I found out why everyone was treating me the way they were. The accusing officer had taken the entire story and turned it around to make me the one responsible for accusing another officer of drinking on duty. Oh, his details were correct, only he flipped it around so that I was making the accusations. It turned out to be my word against his. I was cleared of all but one minor departmental procedure and transferred to another assignment within the department. The transfer was not disciplinary, but because the accusations had involved so many people, they thought it best. What they really meant was the other officer had been in that section for ten years and was having serious marital problems. I, in turn, was new, and a woman, so I was dispensable. I only had contact with the person involved one other time, and I remained professional even though I wanted to punch him out.

To this day, I don't know how that officer could live with himself. Had he fessed up to his responsibilities right from the start, he probably would have been given a reprimand. Instead, he took me down as his scapegoat. Although some people were on my side, there are truly only two people that know what happened that night, he and I, and I hope that one day he decides to make peace and clear his conscience. I could have forgiven him if he told the truth, but he put a blemish on my clean record. It's a blemish that has never healed, and I hope he loses sleep over it.

If I hadn't loved the job so much, these things would have consumed me. But there are negative things in every job. You just have to push against those who want to bring you down and thrive on the positive aspects that make you want to work that much harder.

NOT WHAT THEY SEEM

You would never guess that elderly people can be as difficult and unpredictable as teenagers, but they can. I have always had a soft spot in my heart for the elderly. Maybe it's because I grew up with grandparents we saw regularly, or maybe it's because older people have so many life experiences to share, and they tell it like it is. Whatever the case, the county I worked in offered a lot of wonderful services to the residents. One such luxury was housing for the elderly. Along with assisted living facilities and nursing homes were beautiful residential neighborhoods for the over-fifty-five crowd.

Once in a while, we would get a call from one of these neighborhoods because someone had wandered off or someone had something significant stolen. On one warm spring evening, we received a call from an assisted living facility that a seventy-six-year-old man had gone for a walk and hadn't returned. The man took heart medication and had missed one dose by this time. It was getting dark, and the staff seemed to be getting worried. While a few of my officers were out looking for him, I questioned the staff about his daily routine and friends and family members he had in the area. Sometimes a person will get a whim to go see a family member and hop on a bus and end up quite a distance away. One of the staff members told me the name of a female friend of the gentleman who may know something.

We went to her apartment, and she was not home either. I then started to drive through the neighborhoods trying to guess where these two people might go if they had gone for a walk and gotten lost or ill. Outside of the grounds was nothing but busy neighborhoods. It was hard to imagine that something could have happened to them without someone noticing. There were plenty of homes to knock on if they had needed help.

I was driving very slowly when I saw an elderly man in shorts and a T-shirt come out of a yard holding the hand of an elderly woman. The man walked up to my car, hunched down, and whispered as if he had some huge secret. He said, "Could you give us a ride, Officer? We took a walk and decided to play hooky, and I am afraid we are going to be in big trouble."

The two got into the back of my cruiser and laughed all the way back to their residences. I had radioed ahead to let the staff know I had located our two missing persons, and as we drove up to the main building, the director, who was standing with both hands on her hips, greeted us. The gentleman said, "Uh oh, Lillian. Mrs. Jennings looks mad," and the two laughed out loud. I told Mrs. Jennings not to be too hard on them. It was a beautiful spring evening, and the two had enjoyed a wonderful time pretending to be juveniles again.

3

Shift Work, Night Work, and More Shift Work

When I first joined the police department, we worked seven days and had two off. The first shift was midnights (11:00 PM to 7:00 AM); the second was evenings (3:00 PM to 11:00 PM); and the third was day work (7:00 AM to 3:00 PM). My body never knew which way to go. Two days was never enough time for my body to adjust from sleeping at night to sleeping during the day, and I never knew whether to eat breakfast or dinner.

Holidays meant nothing to most of us when we first started, because we worked all of them. We learned to celebrate Christmas, birthdays, and all other holidays on another day. If a cop is single, this isn't so bad, but if she is married with children, it becomes increasingly difficult. That is why I waited so long to get married and have kids. I was totally into my job when I first came on. Nothing else mattered.

I hated working midnights. No matter how much sleep I tried to get, 4:00 am would come around, and I would want to crash. When that happened and the streets were quiet, we were supposed to buddy up with someone and talk to keep ourselves awake for a while. One time I remember sitting at a stop sign waiting for it to turn green. It never did, of course. I don't think I ever fell asleep on the job, but one time I was sitting in a parking lot when that 4:00 am whistle blew, and I heard my number come out over the radio. I acknowledged the call but later was told they had called me three times before I answered up. I still don't know if they were just messing with me. Though I don't think I ever fell asleep while working, I did fall asleep driving home on two different occasions. The first time was after the last night of midnights, and the second time was after a sixteen-hour shift when I lived an hour and a half from work. After the second accident, we moved. It wasn't worth risking my life to live out in the country.

If the streets were busy, staying awake was no problem. We got a second wind, and sometimes a third or fourth. If we didn't, we could have gotten hurt or made some serious mistakes. That, along with the fact that officers working shift work tended to get sick easily, was why the department went to permanent shifts. Ten hour shifts, four days a week was a lot better than seven straight days of one shift followed by seven of another. Officers took fewer sick days and were more content because most people were able to pick the shift they wanted.

∾

Weather was never an excuse for not making it to work. If an officer couldn't get out of his neighborhood because of snow or the fact that he had to own a Mustang convertible (like many cops) that couldn't get out of a good rain, we would go and get him. Chains would have to be put on, and all four-wheel drive vehicles were put on the street. The only calls we would answer involved life and death or traffic issues. That was all we had time for. More than once, I was stuck at work for two or three days because not enough personnel from the relieving shift could make it in. I always came prepared with an overnight bag and change of uniform. If we worked more than two shifts in a row, the department would put us up at a local motel. If we were lucky, we could dine at the nearest 7-Eleven unless that was closed, too. In that case, thank goodness for vending machines. You can probably see where I am going with this: it's bad enough if you are a man and your wife is stuck at home with the kids, but what if you are a woman with children and your husband is also stuck at work?

4

WHEN IT'S HOT, IT'S HOT

Although a police officer's day has its hours of mundane activity, such as filling out paperwork or driving around neighborhoods, in a department the size of Fairfax County, we saw our share of exciting situations. No two days were ever the same, and we never knew exactly what we were getting into.

One Sunday afternoon, I heard a call go out for a fight at the Jefferson Library. I was almost directly in front of it, so I let the dispatcher know and pulled into the parking lot. The first thing that crossed my mind was that the library wasn't open on Sundays, so this must involve a couple of guys in the parking lot. The dispatcher then advised that there were several people involved in a fight, and bottles were being thrown. As I drove around, it was apparent that either this was not the location or the call was fictitious. I told the dispatcher to check the location. After a minute or so, she told me that it was actually at the Jefferson High School soccer field. I was several minutes away from there, so I hauled freight down the interstate to the school, clocking my speedometer at one hundred and twenty miles per hour. Sure enough, there were about two hundred angry soccer fans throwing bottles, swinging chains, and fighting in the middle of the field. And, of course, there was me.

I called for reinforcements, including state police. When we got into the crowd, most of them took off running, except for the ones who lay bloodied in the field and needed immediate attention. Several of them were gang members from a nearby town who were feuding with our local gang members. Imagine that.

I went for one of the bloodied ones who had been hit several times with a chain. He was alert and not bleeding too badly, so I told him that rescue was enroute and went on to the next poor soul who had been stuck in the shoulder with a broken bottle. It's funny how gang members can't recall who assaulted them. All of the victims were less than cooperative. They preferred to handle the situation themselves, later down the road.

I alerted the hospital that we were bringing several victims in and that many of them were gang members. We had an agreement with the hospital to alert them in such instances so that they could go to a lock down mode if they felt it was necessary to ensure that no rival gang members decided to go to the hospital to finish what they had started. All in all, we treated six persons. Several others had been seen fleeing the area in cars prior to our arrival. Many more of those required medical attention also, but they probably figured they would rather get it somewhere else than risk being locked up. Because no one wanted to talk, no arrests were made. I am sure it was handled between the groups on another day.

૯ૐ

If you have ever heard of a "rave," you know they are parties that you don't want your sons or daughters to go to. Ever. For any reason. They involve a huge number of people in a small dance hall or auditorium. Frequently, Ecstasy is the drug of choice, and sometimes alcohol is available as well. The music is extremely loud to enhance the euphoric effects of the drug. There is usually a light show that helps stimulate the senses while the kids are hallucinating. After a few of these raves were held in our county, the police department persuaded the board of supervisors that they could not allow them anymore. One particular party was billed as a "dance" at the Boys and Girls Club. When the call came in that the dance had spilled into the street and people were fighting and being thrown into windshields, I once again called the cavalry. My thinking was that if enough of us showed up at one time, they would probably disperse on their own without too much of a fight. We were far outnumbered, so we had to let the little things like being drunk in public go and only make arrests if absolutely necessary.

We took five or so to jail for breaking windows and assault and another couple to the hospital for drug overdoses and shut the "dance" down. The parking lot was empty in about forty-five minutes, and none of my guys were hurt, so it was a good night.

Getting hurt from time to time is an inevitable part of the job. I was never seriously hurt, although I had been kicked, punched, thrown down, and even attacked in an elevator. Yes, an elevator. Our jail was several stories high, and we would book our prisoners through the bottom level, go before the magistrate, and then lead them up the elevator to the incarceration desk. We always secured our weapons in the garage before taking the prisoners out of our cruisers, and sometimes, if everything had gone all right, I would take the handcuffs off the prisoner for the ride upstairs. I don't even remember what I had this man for, but the arrest had gone fine and the guy was cooperative throughout, but when we got into the elevator of the jail, he decided to wig out. He began making threatening remarks like, "You don't have your gun now do you? You don't even have a nightstick. I should probably take you out right here."

Now this guy wasn't drunk, he wasn't on drugs, and he obviously wasn't too bright to try and pick a fight with a cop who had about six hundred deputies at the other side of the elevator door. So what happened next? I pushed the intercom button and advised the sheriff's deputies that I might need some assistance soon. Just then, the elevator abruptly stopped, and we were stuck between floors. What are the chances, right? The guy tried to grab me, and I blocked his arm the best I could in the confines of the elevator. He went one way, and I went another until he dropped me halfway to the ground. I pushed the intercom button again and advised them that I was having difficulty with my prisoner and the elevator seemed to be stuck. (I didn't quite say it that way, but this is a PG-rated book.) The deputy acknowledged me, and within sixty seconds or so, the doors opened up, and I shoved my prisoner out into the waiting arms of at least twenty deputies. It was a beautiful sight. Justice was done. I learned never to take the handcuffs off of anyone until I was standing at the cellblock doors.

ᴇᴏ

Usually the most exciting things happen after a lull in the shift. Our county surrounded the Lorton Reformatory, which was a federal prison with three separate facilities: maximum, medium, and minimum security. Our responsibility was to handle the perimeter in the event of an escape or riot. We would provide K-9 units and a helicopter when requested, and we had orders to shoot if a prisoner came over the fence.

One night I was on a routine alarm call at an industrial area that backed up to the prison when a very strange call came over the radio. A person had broken in to the prison, shot and killed a prisoner, and then broke back out. When the call came out, I was walking through the woods with no light but my flashlight not half a mile from the prison. Suddenly, this "routine alarm" wasn't routine anymore. Could the person who committed the prison murder now be the one setting off this alarm in an effort to hide? I was fully awake now, I assure you! Within a few minutes, a lookout was broadcast for a red Mustang. A few hours before, an alert guard had taken down the tag number of a car that appeared disabled near the prison. An officer from my squad checking area roads located the vehicle on a major highway that led into Washington DC. Normally he was very cool and calm, but when he came on the radio, his voice had gone up several octaves. The car had four suspects, and the dispatcher was warning that all could be armed with automatic weapons. At the time, we were still carrying .38-caliber handguns, which were no match for semiautomatic weapons. The officer was told to keep back and follow until appropriate numbers of backup could be detailed. After about ten minutes, there were fifteen or twenty of us, including Virginia State Police, slowing the vehicle down and blocking it in. The vehicle came to a stop, and the occupants were ordered out. After what seemed like an eternity, all occupants came out with their hands up. We recovered four semiautomatic weapons. I am sure the wait entailed a discussion among the bad guys as to whether or not they felt they could win a gun battle. In the end, we probably all would have lost. A couple days later, we learned that one of the gunmen had tuberculosis, and we all had to be tested in case we had contracted it.

This is a very real part of the job: trying to avoid disease that can come from the lower element that police officers often deal with. We get punched, kicked, and spat on more times than you can shake a stick at, and it isn't very pleasant. I had once taken a girl into custody at a mental hospital to transport her to another mental facility. As I was putting her in the back of my cruiser, she turned and spit in my eye. I had barely said a word to her, and I wasn't the reason she was where she was. For a few weeks, I had to undergo treatment and counseling because it was believed that she had AIDS. It was later confirmed that she didn't have AIDS, but it wasn't a very fun experience to go through.

I had another interesting evening at Lorton Reformatory when a homicide detective and I went in to help investigate the "shank" murder of an inmate. (A shank is a homemade knife frequently made of sharpened eating utensils or other materials found in prisons.) I had never been inside the walls of the medium-security prison before. As we walked through the halls, I couldn't believe the conditions. Brick walls had holes in them that could easily hide weapons, drugs, etc. Inmates were passing us so closely that we almost brushed up against them. Suddenly, I felt myself grabbing hold of my male partner saying, "Richard, don't get too far away." As we made our way back to the interview room, passing dozens of inmates quietly talking or just looking at us with cold, dark eyes, Richard and I discovered something almost simultaneously: they weren't looking at me; they were looking at my partner. I felt Richard grab my arm and say, "Connie, don't get too far away." We laughed about that nervously, and I didn't exhale till we got back to our cruiser.

Unfortunately, cases are not frequently solved in an hour like they are on television. For one thing, officers handle many different cases in a shift and usually cannot devote all their time solving one crime. But, sometimes, they can.

A young woman walked into the police station one evening to report that she had been raped. The woman relayed the facts in detail, saying she had been walking near a wooded area, and a man had stopped his car just in front of her and gotten out. With very little said, the man had forced the woman into the woods and raped her. He then had apologized and left.

After getting a full statement and description of the man and vehicle, a sex crimes detective and I drove the woman to the area she had reported to look for a crime scene. After searching for about five or ten minutes, we found an area that looked as if the brush had been disturbed. Lying two feet away was a man's wallet. Inside was a driver's license belonging to a man that not only matched the description given by the victim but lived only blocks away.

We took the young woman to the hospital for an examination to confirm the crime. We then went to the apartment indicated on the driver's license, knocked on the door, and heard a man answer, "Come in." The detective went to one side of the door and I to the other, and with weapons drawn, we pushed open the door. Peering inside, we saw a man sitting on a couch in front of a coffee table covered with lit candles. He had an open Bible in his hands. The man looked up at us saying, "I was sitting here praying that you would come and get me." The detective and I looked at each other, trying not to smile, and took the man into custody. He gave a full statement citing a recent marriage breakup, alcohol, and opportunity as his motives. Case opened and closed within seven hours.

Those kinds of cases are rare, and some cases are not what they first appear. The body of a thirty-five-year-old man was found in his living room by his wife when she came home from work. He had been shot several times, and there was blood all over the house indicating a struggle or attempt to get away. Of course, the wife became "a person of interest" when she told investigators that she had recently asked her husband for a divorce and that financial issues had become a major burden for the couple. After collecting evidence at the scene, an autopsy was scheduled for the next morning.

This was my first autopsy. I had heard that the worst part was the smell, so I tried to keep a little distance from the body while still being able to see what I needed to see. I soon discovered that in order to avoid the smell my distance would have needed to be about one hundred feet. The man had three gunshot wounds: one to the left hand, one to the side of the head, and one to the chest. The medical examiner was able to assist us in determining the events that had occurred in the house based on the damage that was done with each shot. The man was despondent over the impending breakup of his marriage. He took some antidepressants and shot himself in the hand (probably to see what it was like). He then went downstairs to the living room, sat on the couch, and shot himself in the right side of the head. Unfortunately for him, the bullet went through the skull but did not enter the brain, which would have caused his death. The man walked around the house for several hours (based on blood loss and evidence at the scene) before finally taking another shot to the chest. This shot penetrated the heart, causing instant death. What appeared to be a suspicious death turned out to be a suicide.

Forensics is amazing to me. In my next life, I am either going to go into forensics or be a profiler. I love piecing together the puzzle.

જ

One night my training officer and I were dispatched to a vacant house. A neighbor had seen lights and people around. I was told to cover the front while the veteran officer went around back. I heard a commotion inside but didn't know what was going on. Suddenly, four people came running out the front door toward the garage. I ordered them to stop and drew my weapon. The four people—two boys and two girls, all in their late teens—stopped. One of the boys had a knife on the side of his belt, which I ordered him to drop. He slowly took the knife out and held it by the blade. As he raised his arm to throw it at me, I could feel my finger pulling back on the trigger. Something inside of me must have felt he was not going to throw it, because I didn't shoot him. But the kid did throw the knife; luckily it stuck in the ground by my feet. Just then, the other officer came around the corner, and we handcuffed them all. It seems that they had broken into the house to have sex. The boys were eighteen, and the girls were sixteen. The one boy will never know how close he came to dying that night. And for what? I would have been justified. When I told my training officer what had happened, he yelled at me for not shooting him. Dammed if you do, and damned if you don't.

HOME ALONE

I call this my "home alone" case because it reminds me of the Macaulay Culkin movie in which his parents accidentally leave him at home while getting ready for a trip. The difference is that in my case, the son was left alone on purpose.

The call came in to assist the fire department in making forced entry to a home. They had received a 911 hang-up call from the residence. When they got to the house, which was located in an older, well-established neighborhood, all the doors were locked, but one of the medics saw someone push back the curtains from the living room window. We tried all the windows and doors before deciding to make forced entry. After announcing ourselves and giving the person inside one more chance to come out with his hands up, I tried the front door again and found it had been unlocked.

I slowly made entry into the house, tripping over things I couldn't identify in the dark. I announced myself, and a voice came from the opposite side of the room: "I'm here." I turned to find what looked like an eight-year-old boy, sitting on the couch and holding a large bouquet of balloons. He said his name was Tommy and that he was the only person at home. He said his mother was in New Mexico, and his father was at work. I had a medic sit with him while I checked the rest of the house.

The living room was full of dirty dishes, a month's worth of newspapers and magazines, dirt, and about ten different flower arrangements. The kitchen had the remnants of someone's ill attempt at baking cookies. Two trays of burnt cookies lay on the counter along with weeks' worth of slop left on the counters, cupboards, and floor. Papers were everywhere. It looked like an accountant's desk at tax time.

The family room was much the same. It had to have taken a great deal of time and effort to get the house that filthy. I went upstairs to the bedrooms and found all the doors closed. I paused outside for a second, thinking that this kid looked to have been on his own for some time. Could the parents be dead in the house? There was a car in the driveway. So far, everything about this call was bizarre.

I slowly walked up the stairs and stopped to listen for a while. I took the first door on the right, as it looked like it might be a master bedroom. I slowly opened the door while calling out, "Police officer."

The room was in the same disarray as the rest of the house but had no signs of a human being, dead or alive. I did the same to bedroom number two with the same results. When I got to bedroom number three, I heard a buzzing sound. As I opened up the door, the sound got louder. It was a dehumidifier, which helped to blow the stench of filthy clothes, dead fish in an aquarium, and what appeared to be animal feces, although I never found a dog. After clearing the house of any other living being, I took a moment to catch my breath outside and then went back in to talk with "junior."

It was apparent that little Tommy had some sort of mental disability. He turned out to be fourteen, although he looked and acted like an eight-year-old. Little Tommy had been left alone for possibly a couple of weeks and got bored. He used Dad's credit card number to order flowers, balloons, pizza, and even a limo. That in itself was a bit odd, but wait until you hear what he had done the day before we got there.

I went to a few neighbors asking if they had seen parents around or had any background on the family. As I was walking down the street, a car pulled up, and a woman got out. She was the realtor for the owners of the house across the street from Tommy's. The family had already moved away, and she wanted to find out why I was in the area because she had a little story of her own to tell. It seems she had gotten a bill from a tree-cutting firm in the amount of $16,000. The firm had been hired by the "owner" of the house that was for sale to cut down all the trees in the yard and haul them away. The trees were all more than twenty years old. I contacted the firm and was told that an "elderly woman" had called them requesting the service. She had told them that she was handicapped, so she would not be able to come to the door but would watch them from the window. She would happily pay them when the work was done. They came. They cut. And they hauled away about fifteen twenty-year-old, perfectly healthy trees while little Tommy watched and grinned from the window across the street. Well, now we knew that little Tommy wasn't as slow as he seemed, and he did have the voice of an old woman. Next it was time to track down Dad.

After searching papers in the kitchen and calling numbers on the bulletin board, I finally got a cell phone number for Dad. I left a message for him to call his house as soon as possible. In the meantime, I was trying to explain to Social Services why I needed them to come to this house on a Friday afternoon at five o'clock. When Dad called back, I expected him to say, "Who are you, why are you in my house, and where is my son?" Instead, I got, "Well, I can't come home right now; I have to work." He wasn't out of town, just at work some thirty miles away.

I asked him if the house was normally in such disarray. (You have to be careful how you word these things so as not to offend the slobs of the world.) He said, "Well, what do you mean by disarray?" I said food everywhere, newspapers all over the house, dirty clothes piled up, and a stench that would kill a buffalo. His avoidance of the question gave me the answers I needed. He tended to avoid specifics about his son as well, only saying that he was immature for his age. I asked him if he knew that little Tommy was using his credit card. His ears perked up a little bit but not as much as I had expected. The conversation ended with me saying, "You need to be here in one hour to meet with a social worker about your son and your lack of good housekeeping skills. Oh, and your neighbors across the street who have their house on the market? They may want a word with you, too." Not too long after, I heard that the family had moved away. It seems that the parents worked and travelled a lot and would frequently leave their son alone. I never checked on the case further, as we have so many cases to follow up on, but I am sure social services would have charged the parents with neglect and monitored the family for years to come.

5

I CAN BRING HOME THE BACON

...

After seven years on the job, I married another cop. Now as far as he was concerned, he gave me a couple opportunities to visit the emergency room when he was injured rather seriously on two different occasions.

The first time, he and I had been carpooling, and I got to his station to find most of the officers gone. The few who were left looked at me funny but didn't say anything. I went into the report room and asked the supervisor where my husband was. He asked, "Don't you know?" Ron (my husband) was hurt. Apparently, they tried to catch me before I left my station to tell me, but I had already gone, so by the time I had gotten to his station, everyone thought I knew what had happened. The supervisor assured me it wasn't serious and that Ron would be okay.

I went racing up to the hospital, and all I saw were police cruisers. Not serious, huh? I went into the emergency room and grabbed the nearest nurse. I was still in uniform and asked the whereabouts of the cop who was hurt. She said that he was in room one, but I would have to wait; there were already enough police officers in there. I said, "Wait nothing. I am his wife! Kick out some of those other cops!"

It turned out that Ron, who had been patrolling the vast number of bike paths in the area on a dirt bike, had responded to an accident on his way back to the station to help with traffic. Afterward, he couldn't get the dirt bike to start up. He then slammed his boot down hard on the kickstart, which flew back up, penetrated his boot, and stuck in his leg just below the knee. He had to pull the kickstart out of his leg as his boot filled up with blood. He was out of commission for a while.

The second time, I was at home in bed when I heard a commotion downstairs. Ron came crawling up the stairs with a cast and crutches. Several neighborhood pools had been vandalized in recent weeks. Officers were staking out a couple of them when a group came by breaking bottles and throwing furniture in the pool. Ron started to chase one of the bad guys in the pitch black that night, when both he and the bad guy went over a cliff. Both landed on huge rocks. Ron's left leg went one way, his knee went another, and his right ankle became wedged in between two rocks. He grabbed hold of the bad guy who was feeling a little pain himself until help could arrive. His backup officers came looking for him and heard him yelling from below the cliff. He never let go of the prisoner until other officers took custody of him.

Now I had my husband home again with two injured legs. Can you feel my pain? I had two children to care for and a job myself. After a few days, I had to get back to work for a break. I would get up early in the morning, pack him a cooler, and get him situated in an easy chair or bed before

I left for the day. Sometimes I look back at those times and wonder how it all managed to come together.

Neither of us have ever been shot or stabbed and we have never shot another person ourselves. Thank God. I attribute that to our excellent training. A police related shooting in our county is a rare thing.

Besides the kid I almost shot for throwing a knife at me, the only other time I came close to shooting someone turned out to not be a person at all. I was dispatched to a rape that had just occurred in a brand new townhouse complex. The victim told the call-taker that the man had just left on foot. It was about three o'clock in the morning on a windy, cold autumn day. I walked around the corner of the townhouse just as a gust of wind blew a huge piece of plastic from the construction area right in front of me. I think if we had been issued 9 mm weapons at that time, the plastic would have been dead. Instead, it lived to scare another person half to death as it continued on across the parking lot.

This is probably just as good a place as any to accent the problems of being a female police officer. I gained fifty-two pounds when I was pregnant with my son. I was fortunate enough to have an indoor job during the time I was pregnant and just so happened to have gotten promoted during that time as well. It all went great until I returned to work afterward.

I was nervous anyway because I was now a new sergeant being transferred to a new station after having been on maternity leave for three months. I wanted to make a good impression with the new squad, so I got to work early and got everything ready. When it came time to put the uniform on, it hit me. I had never requested larger pants. I only had my pre-baby size sixes.

"Oh, God!" I had to be on time for roll call. I had to go in completely in uniform. I had to look cool, calm, and in control. "Oh, God! My milk is coming in!" Sure as hell, I was so nervous and that five-pound bulletproof vest hit my nipples, and the milk was on! My T-shirt was saturated, my pants wouldn't zip, my gun belt didn't have any more notches in it, and I had three minutes to get into roll call. So, I did what any red-blooded woman would do. I sucked it in like never before, calmly walked into roll call, introduced myself to the troops, and exhaled for the first time thirty minutes later. The next day, I went up to the property room and got what I called "crisis pants." I loved the job and never regretted getting into law enforcement, but like most mothers, it was difficult to leave my new baby.

In all fairness, though, there are good points to being a female officer too. In what other profession can you have a thousand "big brothers"? In what other job can you go up to some two hundred-pound man, slap handcuffs on him, and tell him he is under arrest? In what other job can you pretend to be a hooker and watch the look on the john's face when he finds out you're a cop? It's great! I'm telling you! There is nothing like it in the world.

∾

We had received several complaints from a local motel that hookers—both men and women—had been coming and going pretty regularly. We got the name of the local "service" and gave them a call. We said that we were a group of ladies at a bachelorette party and asked them to send us a male stripper. We had to make it look like we were really having a party, so we put a bunch of open chip bags around, some empty beer bottles, cranked up some music, and had one of the girls blow some smoke around to make it look like we were party girls. Our "stripper" showed up and asked us what we would like. Well, a dancing stripper would be nice. We introduced our fake bride-to-be, and he proceeded to dance around while taking his clothes off. He offered "other services," and after money changed hands, we stopped him before he took it all off and announced that we were all cops and he was under arrest for prostitution. I didn't know a man's jaw could actually touch the ground until that night.

പ

We had also had frequent complaints of underage parties where alcohol was being sold and a "cover charge" was required. This type of party was very popular and frequently involved clueless or uncaring parents. My job was to pay a cover and go in and make a visual on the person taking the money, the one giving out alcohol, and any adults in the area. At one such party, I attempted to get the person who was taking the money to walk to the door with me. I was soon "made," and two males attempted to hold me back so the kid could make a getaway. I broke loose and ran outside in pursuit of my "collar" (arrest). I got on my hidden radio and told the troops in the area that I was in foot pursuit and needed assistance. The only thing my "heroes" saw was kids running, so they grabbed the nearest ones they could reach. One of those they grabbed was me! They had gotten me confused with the kids. I was yelling and laughing at the same time. "Not me, you idiot, get them!" It's all good.

പ

I wanted to do it all, and I wanted to do it all well. Sometimes it worked, and sometimes it didn't.

I would do things around the house at odd hours, so I could be with my kids on my days off. I wallpapered my kitchen at three o'clock in the morning. I made Halloween costumes all night and would tidy up around the house until midnight. I was once told I had to "deduct points" for setting an impossible example for everyone else. But that kind of routine couldn't go on forever. The fact is that law enforcement and family don't always mix well. When I came on the police force, the department didn't want an officer to have any life other than work. It was all lip service when they said, "Family comes first." It was clearly not the case.

The job is stressful and unpredictable. The hours are long, and I could have easily spent a day or two in court on my scheduled days off. If you are a father and a cop and you find yourself in a child-care predicament, everyone says, "Oh, poor Joe. Let's give him a hand," and everyone pitches in. If you are a mom and a cop and you get into a child-care predicament, everyone says, "You can't handle both; you should be at home with the kids." So what do you do with childcare? You have three options: rely on family, quit, or hire live-in childcare. I had no family available to care for my kids. Quitting was discussed but ruled out. So option number three became the only viable option for us as a two-cop family.

I hated the idea of a stranger being in our house all the time; my husband couldn't walk around in his underwear, and we had to incorporate this person into our lives. In nine years, we had ten nannies. We had the best, and we had the worst.

Mary Poppins and Mr. Belvedere were already taken. So, I had to go through the endless task of interviewing people who might be suitable for the position. I found that most nannies were young girls either looking to see another part of the world or trying to get away from something. We couldn't go the au pair route, because our hours were too unpredictable. We couldn't guarantee only forty hours a week. So, I had to look on the domestic front.

I spoke to an agency, gave them the outline of our needs, and let her go to work looking for someone suitable. Our first nanny was a nineteen-year-old girl from Illinois named Vonna, who started out okay but then decided she liked the nightlife that the Washington DC area had to offer a little too much. She was often out all night and would sleep all day. She would always be on the phone, and her phone bills were $300 to $400 per month. I took this out of her paycheck, which didn't leave her with a whole lot. (In case it hasn't hit you yet, live-in childcare is very expensive.) The final straw with her was when I got up at three o'clock in the morning to go to work, and she wasn't home yet. She snuck in while I was in the shower, hoping I wouldn't notice. I noticed. Vonna was put on a bus back to Illinois.

Next came Olga. She was a thirty-two-year-old woman who had been caring for other families' kids but liked the idea of having three days off in a row with us. Olga was fine too, for a while, until things started to disappear, and her "legal problems" with a former husband took precedence. Olga was told to pack up.

Then there was Barbara. Barbara was an overweight fifty-six-year-old African-American woman with a great sense of humor who loved kids and loved to cook. It sounded like it would work out beautifully. The only catch was that Barbara wanted to live with her grown kids in Washington DC, so I would have to pick her up the day before my shift at the Metro, some thirty miles away, and then take her back again.

This was draining, but my priority was good childcare. I had the chance to meet Barbara's family when they all came out to our house one day.

Everything seemed to be just fine until Barbara didn't show up at the Metro station one day. It took me an entire day to track down her daughter who told me her mom thought the travel back and forth was too much, so she needed to quit. I never heard from Barbara. She left all her belongings at my house, kissed the kids good-bye at the Metro, and we never saw her again.

You are probably getting the drift by now that it hasn't been a real smooth life so far in regards to childcare. Somehow or another, my kids came out of it unscathed, probably because they were too little to remember. Thank God.

After Barbara, came Veronique. Veronique was French and certainly the most interesting experience we had (interesting in the sense that we all somehow lived through it). Veronique spoke pretty good English and was very willing to learn. She was nineteen and in awe of being in the United States. At the time, Veronique only had to care for my three-year-old son. She was very attentive and seemed to be learning our American ways. Things seemed to be okay for a while. Then strange little things began to happen.

Veronique was not big on personal hygiene. We had to politely mention that she needed to use deodorant and shampoo more often, and we went shopping to get these products. She seemed to like the idea and appeared grateful for the products. But then she started taking showers to the tune of two and three times a day. At first I just thought she was enjoying her newfound interest in cleanliness, but then it went a little too far. I would come home from work to find her wearing my clothes. Not just any clothes, but clothes from the dirty laundry basket—layers of them. When I would say something, she would look down in surprise and laugh and go change like she was confused as to how they got on her.

Then other strange things started to happen. My husband came home from work one night about one o'clock in the morning, and Veronique was sitting in front of the open refrigerator and talking to the food. She started to sleep outdoors in a sleeping bag during the day and walking the halls at night. We decided that something unusual must be happening, and we couldn't trust her to be alone with our son.

I took Veronique into town to a travel agency to see if I could send her back to France. While Veronique was pacing the sidewalk outside the office, the agent told me it would cost more than $1,000 to send her back. I told the agent I didn't care if it was a cargo flight; I had to get her out of my home. She said she would do some checking, and we all went home. We contacted the sponsor who refused to help in any way until we threatened to contact the Immigration and Naturalization Service on her to see if her method of bringing girls over from France was completely legal. We got her attention. She said we could bring Veronique over on the weekend, and she would see what she could do.

The weekend was only two days away, so I figured we could manage. We always had our guns locked up, and I had even taken all the cutlery knives out of the house and locked them in my car. I was exhausted the first day because I had worked all night. My husband was doing day work, so I was home alone with my son and the nanny from hell. I locked my son and myself in my bedroom and soon woke to find Veronique standing at the foot of my bed watching me.

I don't know how she got in, but I tried to get my husband on the phone. He couldn't be located, so I fell back to sleep for a while. Without my knowledge, Veronique had taken the phone off the hook.

When my husband got the message that something was wrong at home and he couldn't get through to us, he sent the local police by the house to check on me. Just as they arrived, my husband pulled in. He must have broken speed barriers to get home as fast as he did. We threw all Veronique's belongings into the car and drove her to her sponsor's house in Washington. With that, we said, "See ya," hightailed it to the car, and peeled off out of there. You would think that was where the story ended, but it didn't.

At five o'clock the next morning, a call came from a doctor who spoke French at the psychiatric ward of Georgetown University Hospital. She needed to know all the details as to what was going on. I repeated the events of the past ten months and asked the doctor what was going on with Veronique. She said that Veronique had grown "unnaturally close" to our family.

She thought we had the perfect lives, the perfect marriage, and the perfect child. It was so different from what she had in France that she decided she wanted to be me. That was why she was wearing my clothes and watching me sleep; she wanted to take over. I asked the doctor if she would have eliminated me. The doctor paused for what seemed like an eternity and then said, "Yes. She loved all of you, but you were in the way of her becoming you. So she would have had to eliminate you."

That put a chill up my spine. It all made sense. I hung up the phone and slept for fourteen hours. The next day, the doctor called back and said that she had spoken to

Veronique's parents in France. Veronique had become violent and had to be escorted home to Paris by a doctor and nurse. Six months later, Veronique called us saying she was feeling much better and was out of the mental hospital on weekends and could she have her job back. The word "no" didn't come fast enough.

After that interesting international experience, I decided to go back to domestic nannies. I hired Pam, who was okay for about six months but then had to be sent packing like the others.

At this point, I began to rethink everything. We had hired a lot of young girls, so I started to think that maybe an older person would be more suitable. They were certainly a lot more expensive because they were experienced, but I was willing to pay. We hired Anne. My son was four and a half, and my daughter was nine months. Anne was very German and a bit gruff but sounded like she would fill the void.

As soon as she got off the plane, I didn't like her. She was complaining about the flight and the weather and everything else. I thought perhaps she just needed some time to adjust, so I took a few days off to show her around and help her get into a routine. My first clue that this was a mistake was when we were in my minivan driving the ten miles to town, and she said there was way too much traffic and she would not be able to handle the car. Well, we lived in a rural area. Traffic consisted of twenty other cars within a five mile radius during the time she would have to drive my son to preschool. I realized she wasn't going to work either. I called the agency back within a week of Anne setting foot in Virginia. They said they would look for someone else, and I told Anne I would have to send her back in about a week.

I came home from work one day, and my son was sitting on the front porch looking very sad and asked me, "When is Anne going home?" I asked him why he wanted to know, and he said that Anne was mean to him; she would hit him in the head and send him to his room. Anne was very helpful and caring when I was around, but it seemed that she was quite different when I was gone.

My sisters were going to the beach during this time, so I asked them to take my son so that Anne only had my nine-month-old daughter to care for. I wasn't completely sure that something bad was happening, but I did want to have an extra pair of eyes and ears, so I set up my video camera in such a way that it would be able to record sound. It was too big and clumsy to be set up to film, so I felt the sound was good enough. I would start the camera as I was going out the door, and it would give me two hours of recorded sound. I put a second sound-activated recorder in the nursery to pick up anything that happened in the baby's room. When I got home at about three o'clock the next morning, I did my usual things to get ready for bed and then turned on the camera to listen.

It began right away. My daughter could be heard moving around in her walker on the wooden floors. At times she would make her way toward the kitchen where Anne was on the phone. At one point, she came down the hall making noises like she were about to start crying. Anne began yelling at her saying, "Can't you just let me talk on the phone for five minutes?" She would cuss like a truck driver and then push my daughter in her walker down the hall until she crashed into the wall. Stunned, my daughter would then walk back up the hall making the same noises as if she were about to cry. Again, Anne would shove her down the hall until she hit the wall. Anne would cuss her out and then lock her in the adjoining sun room. The entire two hours of tape consisted of Anne yelling at my infant daughter, forcing food into her mouth, forcing a bottle on her, and telling her she didn't care if she had already had a nap because she was "going to throw her butt in bed."

I was shocked to hear that someone could be so mean for no reason whatsoever. I called to my husband to come and listen to parts of it, but after a few short minutes, he walked away unable to listen to anymore. The recorder that was in the nursery also yielded information when Anne literally threw my daughter into the crib yelling, "Shut up, shut up, shut up," at the top of her lungs. After it was over and I had listened to everything, I went into the bathroom and threw up. It was now five thirty in the morning, and I was exhausted. I went to sleep on the floor in my daughter's room. My husband and I agreed that as soon as we had slept awhile, we were getting Anne out of the house. At about eight o'clock, I woke up, got dressed, and fed my daughter and then called a neighbor and asked if I could bring her over for a few hours while we dealt with Anne.

I told Anne we had recorded everything that went on in the house while we were gone and knew she had been abusing the kids, and she was to leave the house immediately. Her face went totally white. She began to sweat and wipe her forehead constantly. We followed her up to her bedroom and told her to pack everything. Still dressed in her night clothes, we threw her and her belongings into the car and drove her to the airport at ninety miles per hour. At the airport, we threw her and her bags on the curb without a word. We could hear her asking, "How do I get home?"

When we returned home, I called the agency and left an emergency message saying we had trouble, and I had gotten it all on tape. A couple of days later, the agency told me that Anne had been stuck at the airport for twenty-four hours before she could get a flight home. Once home, she told her family what we had done, and they admitted her into the hospital for "heart palpitations." They threatened to sue us. I had the tapes transcribed and sent them to the agency to verify my story. They took them to the family for them to listen to and read. We never heard from them again. The agency worked hard to have Anne blackballed in Iowa. The attorney general of Iowa at the time, who was big on child rights, got involved and introduced legislation to require nannies to submit to a national registry, which would prevent people like Anne from ever working in the same capacity again. Luckily, my kids have no recollection of Anne. I can only hope that what goes around comes around.

By now I was getting pretty good at this nanny interviewing thing but still bad at picking out the good ones. When I hired Janet, I told her all that I had been through and that I wasn't going to go through it again. I further added that I would video tape when and where I wanted, and if I even suspected that my children were being mistreated, I would bury her body so far in the woods that no one would ever find her. She took the job despite my threats, so I figured she couldn't be all bad. Janet was very bubbly, a little strange perhaps, but she cared for the kids. The obvious pattern here is that good nannies only last for about a year. Then they go back to school, go back to a boyfriend, or go to a mental institute. Janet went back home a year later. My husband and I didn't expect anything more after this.

Sheila also came from Iowa. She had a lot of energy and was very playful with the kids. She also got along the best with my husband, which was no easy task. My husband could be very intimidating, and he spoke his mind and spoke it often. Sheila was able to laugh at him, something no one else had dared do before. Sheila was also a good cook, and when Ron would bring home a rabbit or squirrel or other such kill, she would cook it up in such a way that even Ron would be impressed. She did, however, question her contract when he asked her to help him hang a dead deer in the garage.

Sheila took on a new career after two years and remains a good friend to this day. She was good to the kids, and they liked her. She was the shining star on our nanny adventures. It is a wonderful feeling when you can go to work and know that your kids are safe and happy and well cared for. I can honestly say that Sheila was the first to give me that relief.

Still another nanny named Katrin could not easily be forgotten. She was from Estonia. Katrin was a little tense sometimes, and little things to me would seem major to her. None of my nannies called me at work much, probably because they knew I was tough to reach but also because they knew it would throw me into a panic. One such call was made, however, when I was en route to a "possible suicide attempt, man with a gun in a hallway apartment."

As the supervisor in charge, I would never send an officer into a situation that I would not go in to myself. I had two or three officers on the scene when I got a message to call Katrin. Thinking that something critical must have happened, I picked up my cell phone and started to dial. Just as I was pulling into the apartment complex, one of the first officers to arrive asked me my status. I told him to wait until I could get up with him before moving in on the apartment. Just then, my phone call went through. Half panicking, I said, "Katrin? What's wrong?" In broken English she said, "Oh, Connie. I just wanted to check with you to see if I could make some cinnamon rolls." I switched to the radio, which was in my left hand, and told the officers I would be up in one minute and then switched to the phone in my right and told Katrin she could go ahead and make cinnamon rolls. That night we had a little discussion about priorities.

I did back up my officers in time. Just as I made it out of the elevator, the suspect came out of the apartment with the gun and gave himself up. I couldn't do everything and do it well.

6

... AND JUSTICE FOR ALL?

Court was always an interesting place to be. Cops either liked it or hated it. It was a meeting place for officers who hadn't seen each other in a while and a place to share stories and catch up on other people's lives. If we were prepared, court was a fun place to go. I liked listening to other people's cases and seeing how other officers testified. I was always prepared because if we weren't, the judge would often make us look like fools, and we would leave with our tails between our legs, vowing never to return unprepared.

Some judges had an afternoon "tee time" that would require them to get through the docket with the speed of a gazelle. If a cop didn't have his radar calibrations or his notes, or he had forgotten to put his gun in the lock box before the judge walked in, he was toast. There was also Senior Citizens Day and other unofficial "holidays" that judges would use to shorten the docket. If the defendant didn't come dressed properly or didn't address the judge with some form of respect, he would often find himself in more hot water than if he had simply paid a fine. And God help the defendants who needed an interpreter. The judge would look at them from the top of his glasses all the while calculating how late he may have to move his "tee time" back.

All the cops knew all the judges, and our day was pretty well determined by which judge we got. Some judges liked to try every speeding case, every accident case, and every radar case as if it were the only case on the docket. If we walked in and saw that one of these judges was on the bench, we knew we'd better hit the restroom and pop a NoDoze, because it was going to be a long day.

Some judges, on the other hand, were a lot of fun. We prayed that we would get one of these if we had a case with a particularly arrogant defendant. One judge in particular would listen to every word the defendant would say, and just about the time the defendant would attempt to insert his foot in his mouth, the judge would ask him if he had brought his toothbrush with him. Usually, the stunned defendant would answer no, and the judge would say, "That's too bad, because I'm sentencing you to two days in jail." Justice would then have been served.

Once I had a case in court that involved a man arrested for being drunk in public for about the hundredth time. All the judges knew his name. He had spent a couple years in jail for various alcohol abuse charges, but he would just get right back into it when he got out. I had been warned by other officers that if I ever came across this guy to watch his feet, because he always kicked. When my turn came to have the honors of locking him up for being drunk in public, he didn't kick; he just kept calling me "cracker."

He would say, "You can't lock me up; you ain't nothing but a cracker." When his name was called in court, I got up as the arresting officer.

After hearing the facts of the case, the judge asked me if I had the man's arrest record. Before I could reply, the judge said, "Nevermind. I know this man, and I know his record. And judging by your size, I think you would need a wheelbarrow to bring it all in here." I was not offended. In fact, I got a chuckle out of it like everyone else in the courtroom. Racism was not a big issue in Fairfax County. We had our bad areas like every other jurisdiction, but those bad areas included a mix of races.

On another day our "humorous" judge announced one of his well known "holidays." If a defendant was older than sixty or drove a certain car, then he would automatically go free. No one ever questioned it. This judge did have a little bit of a problem one day, though, when after listening to an Asian defendant plead his case on a county sticker charge, he sentenced the man to "hang by the neck until dead." Before the man and the rest of the courtroom could gasp, the judge laughed and said, "I'm just kidding. I never forgave you guys for Pearl Harbor." I heard later that the judge had been reprimanded. Judges have a huge amount of power.

One day, purely by accident, my husband and I wound up in the same courtroom at the same time. We knew this could lead to a problem because we were both Lieutenant Novak, but the bailiffs offered to help us out. Sure enough, the same judge that likes to play pranks was on the bench. The judge called for "Novak." One of the bailiffs asked, "Which Novak, sir?"

The judge looked perplexed and said, "Lieutenant Novak."

The bailiff decided to have a little fun with the judge himself and replied," Which Lieutenant Novak, sir?"

The judge took off his glasses, and my husband and I stood up when the bailiff said, "There are two Lieutenant Novaks, sir."

The judge then asked, "When did the two of you get married?" I told him six years prior, and the judge turned to the bailiff and said, "Why doesn't anyone tell me anything around here?"

Judges get to know an officer, even in a department as big as ours. A police officer has to keep her cool at all times and never, never, never compromise her integrity, because that is what the job is all about. If she doesn't get a guilty verdict on all her cases, then she just moves on to the next. You do what you can, and in the end, what goes around comes around. More times than not, the judge will see right through someone who is lying, and the consequences can be severe.

Once in a while, a case would come along where the defendant's testimony was so outrageous it didn't even come close to the truth or remotely resemble the incident I remembered. One time I had a young gentleman in court on a traffic charge, and he was questioning the fact that I had written the ticket using "Sr." after the name. (Apparently I had taken the name off the registration card, which was the same as the driver, only the driver was a junior.) The gentleman stood up with his father and said, "Which one of us did you charge?" I had so many cases on my plate at the time, and this one had occurred about two months prior, so I wasn't sure which one I had charged and told the judge that. The case was dismissed but not without the gentleman and his father getting a tongue lashing from the judge for playing games in his courtroom.

I experienced a feeling of elation when I had the opportunity to put someone away that had broken the law for years and never held a respectable job a day in his life. I was behind a brand new red Corvette at a traffic light one afternoon. For no apparent reason, the car took off through the red light after he had been sitting at it a few seconds. I gave the dispatcher my location and then signaled the man to stop. As I approached the car, it appeared that the driver was somewhat out of sorts. I asked him for his driver's license and registration. The man reached toward the glove box (which in this car was a leather pouch), and I could see the butt of a gun. As I put my gun in his ear and ordered the man not to move, I notified the dispatcher that I needed backup and that weapons were involved. This usually brings out the cavalry. I had about nine backup officers that day.

After taking the man into custody for driving under the influence, a search of his car revealed several pounds of marijuana, hundreds of illegal pills of various kinds, and notebooks showing who he was selling to and who still owed him money—the mother lode, so to speak. I would later learn that this man, who was forty-two years of age, had never held down a job for more than a year, yet he owned his own house and was driving a brand new Corvette. It didn't take a brain surgeon to figure out where the money had come from, and it made my day to see him led out of the courtroom in handcuffs to begin serving his ten-year sentence. It's all a game, but it's more fun when you're the good guy.

7

IT'S THE LITTLE THINGS

My job gave me a great deal of satisfaction. I have a need to feel I am accomplishing something in a positive way, and although some people view police negatively, I think far more respect police and have a positive view of them. I know that was true for my department anyway, and that was why I chose to work for Fairfax County. There were the little things that made the job so much more enjoyable, and sometimes people would go out of their way to show their support.

I stood at a major intersection one freezing February night, directing traffic for eight hours. We had a hostage situation at a local high school where a despondent young man took his ex-girlfriend and a few office staff members into the main offices and held them at gunpoint until he could talk with his girlfriend alone. I had to divert traffic at rush hour from going in front of the school. It's funny how many people only know one way home. You change that route, and their whole life is turned upside down. I don't know how many people stopped in the middle of the road wanting to argue with me about why they had to go a different way. I had to yell at some people, "Find another way home! You can't go down this road. We have an armed man with hostages at the school!" Two people still wanted to argue saying, "I'll drive slowly and just sneak by." God help the ignorant!

I watched a little old lady park on the side of the road. She walked up to me (in the middle of a busy intersection) and explained that she worked for the Red Cross and knew I had been there for a long time and then she offered me a cup of hot coffee. Wow! That blew me away. How nice was that? Only I had never had a cup of coffee in my life—still haven't. I'm probably the only shift worker in the world who hasn't. I thanked the woman for her kindness and told her I didn't drink coffee, only tea, but I appreciated her attempt at making my situation less trying.

No more than half an hour went by when I saw the woman pull over again and get out of her car. She walked up to me with a thermos full of hot tea. She said, "This should work for you. It is hot tea. Just leave the thermos at the police station when you are done with it, and I will pick it up later." I couldn't believe she went so far out of her way to help me out. When I finally got back into my cruiser that night, it was still hot and was the best tea I had ever had.

There was also an elderly gentleman who approached me outside a 7-Eleven store one morning and gave me a lottery ticket. I told him I couldn't accept it, and he looked hurt. He said he bought lottery tickets for police officers whenever he saw them but that he had never bought one for a lady cop before, and he would very much like to do so. Reluctantly, I accepted. The gentleman asked me what color limousine I liked better black, white, or blue. I told him blue and asked why it mattered. He said that when I won the lottery, he would pick me up in a blue limo and drive me to Richmond to pick up my winnings. I got a big laugh out of that. I didn't win, but I did run into him again one day, and he bought me another lottery ticket. He repeated his limo story and then asked me if I wanted to stop by his house and "play a little croquet." I had to graciously refuse his offer, but I later found out that he was quite the croquet player and had even won some state competitions. Those were the little things that helped make the job so satisfying.

Of course, the children are the best. We would get many lost children cases. In almost all of the ones I worked, the children were found within a couple of hours, usually right in the house or at a neighbor's. In one such case, a toddler was missing, which usually would cause concern on everyone's part. Toddlers don't usually venture too far away, so officers are trained to check the house thoroughly first as the child might be just hiding or playing. The mother said she had put the little girl down on the couch for a nap and then gone into the kitchen to start cooking. She was frantic. The child was nowhere to be found. All the neighbors were looking everywhere.

I asked the first responding officer if he had checked the house thoroughly, and he said he had. I went over to the couch where the mother said she had laid the girl to look for anything out of the ordinary. I then got down and looked under the couch. I shined my flashlight and saw the little girl up against the wall, wrapped in the curtain. She was sleeping just fine; she had probably fallen off the couch in her sleep, rolled underneath, and then wedged herself against the wall, getting tangled in the draperies. That was one shocked and happy mom, and the rest of us got a good laugh out of it.

Another day, I responded with my training officer to a report of two missing six-year-olds. It was a very cold autumn night and getting dark, so this one didn't sound good. It was a new housing development, so there were houses under construction and plenty of places to hide. We started with the houses first and then went to the construction areas. We both looked down the hill at a pond but chose not to think about those deadly possibilities. We drove around for a little while and talked about where we would go if we were six years old. The school the girls went to wasn't too far away, so we took a drive down. It was completely dark by now, and we drove out onto the playground. As we began to turn around, our headlights glanced off of two figures running toward the school. We both looked at each other and raced after them. The girls were hiding behind a dumpster in the back of the school.

Not wanting to frighten them, we slowly walked up, and I said, "Girls, how are you? My name is Officer Curran, and this is Officer Flint. We have been looking for two girls named Lisa and Marie. Their parents are very worried and have been looking for them for a long time. Could you be those two girls?" When we got no response, I tried further, "It sure is cold out here tonight, and I would be real happy to take the two of you home so you can warm up." After a few seconds, the girls shyly came from behind the dumpster. I asked, "Are you Lisa and Marie?" They both nodded. I said, "Let's go home, okay?"

We walked them to the car and put them in the back seat. I then got on the radio, which was buzzing with officers checking various locations for the two girls. I said, "I have located the two girls; they are fine. Advise the parents that we are bringing them home." As we rounded the corner where the girls lived, I turned on my flashing blue lights and drove down the street where about fifty people were anxiously awaiting our arrival. It was a very happy reunion, and I left feeling like I was "all that." It seems that the girls had been playing in the neighborhood, and when it started to get dark, they panicked thinking they would get into trouble at home, so they went to the only other place they felt safe—their school. It's a great feeling when a plan comes together. I was tickled at Thanksgiving when I received a card signed by the two girls, thanking me for finding them and bringing them home. I still have that card some thirty years later.

8

SIGNAL 34 SAYS IT ALL

Say what you want about domestic calls, but I think mental cases (signal 34 is the police code) are the worst calls to go on. At least on a domestic call, we can all somewhat relate to what is going on and offer some semblance of sympathy. But who knows what is going on inside the mind of a mental patient? These calls take quite a bit of time, as well. If we get a signal 34, we can count on being tied up for four or six hours on a normal case. If a person threatens suicide or threatens to hurt another person, a police officer can take him into custody for up to six hours to have him evaluated by a mental health official. This is Virginia law. If no doctor or mental health professional deems the person a danger to himself or others, or does not get a mental petition in that period of time, then the person must be cut loose.

It was always a hassle if you had a person injured who had to go to the emergency room. Regular emergency room doctors didn't want to get involved with these cases because they would have to appear in front of a judge the following day to testify as to why they thought the person was a danger.

Doctors don't like court. Hence, the officer has to babysit the person until such time that a mental health professional makes the determination.

I had one emergency room doctor refuse to sign papers for a patient I had brought in because "he didn't have time to appear before a judge." The patient had broken his hand by slamming it into a chest of drawers and then picked up a gun and tried to shoot himself. Lucky for him, his hand was broken, and he wasn't able to bring the gun up close enough to his head; he ended up grazing his temple when the gun was fired. After he was treated for the hand and head injury, I told the doctor that he would have to sign a mental petition. The doctor kept refusing, saying he didn't want to get involved with mental patients, so I explained the law to him. The law stated that I must release him within four hours. We had thirty minutes left; therefore, if the doctor was unwilling to do his job and sign the petition, I would be forced to walk away and let the doctor dwell on the fact that the man would probably be in the hospital's morgue by sunrise. Reluctantly, the doctor signed, and the man was admitted, but police officers have to deal with this type of thing.

℅

The taser was a wonderful invention for law enforcement to deal with mental cases. It looks somewhat like a flashlight, so you can hold it in your hand without a person knowing what it is. If needed, the taser is pointed at a person, a button is pushed, and two darts come out emitting fifty thousand volts of electricity, which renders most people immobile. The down side is you have to be within fifteen feet of a person, and anyone that might be touching the person would also be sent a few jolts.

I came close to experiencing this first hand when I had been on the department for about four years, and my supervisor showed up at the scene of my mental case with a taser. I had a teenage boy who was adamant that he was not going to go with us for a psychiatric evaluation. He was becoming increasingly agitated with our presence, and we knew we would have to fight him. My sergeant pulled out the taser, which I had never seen before, and ordered me to let the boy go. I looked at him quizzically but did what I was told. The sergeant hit the taser button, and both darts penetrated the boy's bare chest, sending him writhing to the ground. Had I still been touching him, I too would have done what became known as the "funky chicken." Tasers were new then but are now carried by most departments.

™

My last patrol area had four or five psychiatric hospitals in it, so we would have at least one psych call per shift. One hospital called us after a patient refused to be sedated and was becoming more and more uncooperative. Normally, the doctor would just get a few orderlies together and take care of the problem, but when they called for us, I knew it had to have a catch.

I was briefed by the first officer on the scene as to the background of the problem. It seemed that the gentleman in question was six feet ten inches tall, weighed 320 pounds, and had been "delivered" to this country in full restraints from Africa after being tasered seven times with no effect. I didn't ask why this man had been delivered from Africa, but I am guessing he was out of control and needed services that were not available to him in Africa. I didn't even want to know the rest of the story. I had heard enough. This man was going to be a problem.

We devised a plan whereby I would talk to the man and try and convince him that the doctor wanted to help him sleep better after such a long journey from home. As I was talking to him, the doctor would slip around back of him and administer the shot wherever she could find a spot. If this failed, it was "best man wins." Either my charm dazzled him or the fact that he saw how little I was compared to him calmed him, because he relaxed after a few seconds, and they hit him in the shoulder with the shot. I don't know what was in that shot, but it had to have been an elephant tranquilizer, because he didn't flinch. My guys and I walked out of the hospital saying thanks to God, because that one could have been a very ugly scene.

෫෮

After you become a supervisor, a lot of the reasons you became a cop tend to fade. You are seldom first on the scene of something, you don't get to investigate cases from beginning to end, and you miss out on a lot of the action—but not always.

I was patrolling around a shopping center and noticed a woman acting strange. She seemed to be talking to herself and moving around very quickly. I called for the area unit to meet me and continued watching her. The woman's movements became wilder as she flailed her arms around and began walking very fast. I felt I should approach her before she or someone else got hurt. I called for the woman to wait for me so I could talk to her, but she turned and looked at me and became more agitated. I drove my car past her and got out so

I would be walking toward her and not trying to chase her down. The woman was almost yelling and continued flailing her arms about. I asked her to stop, and she responded by running toward me and trying to kick me in the shin.

At the time, my son was learning karate, and I would practice moves with him. He would try to kick me, and I would try to intercept his kick, so I put that move into play. I moved to the side and grabbed her leg, taking her off balance, and she slammed into the window of a video store and then to the ground with such a thud that I thought she was dead. She didn't move for a few seconds as several people gathered at the video store window to watch. Then her eyes opened, and she was as angry as an alley cat. I jumped on her and got her on her stomach so I could get handcuffs on her. Just then, my backup arrived. This officer was an avid bodybuilder and came over laughing, saying, "How did you do that? I'm impressed. I thought you killed her." I whispered that I did too, and we got her kicking and screaming into the back of my cruiser where she was transported to jail for assault on a police officer. They in turn put her in the psych unit where she had been before. It was nice to hear my backup describe to the rest of the squad how the "Lieutenant knocked out a nut who was trying to take her out."

Another time I was sent to a house where an officer was out with a mentally ill person. This woman was about sixty-five years old, five feet eight inches, and two hundred pounds and was refusing to go with her family to a psychiatric ward for an evaluation. A mental health professional had evaluated her previously and determined that she was a danger to herself and others, so a judge ordered papers for her committal. It's always better, however, if the person goes voluntarily. This was not going to be one of those easy cases.

A person her age could get hurt if we tried to take her into custody using force. Several of us tried to talk her into it, but we were not getting anywhere, so I made the decision that we would take her forcibly. I told her for the final time that she could go with us voluntarily, or we would have to use force. She seemed to be willing to go but said she wanted to take her slippers off and put on shoes that were in the kitchen.

We followed her in, and as she was changing her shoes, I turned to talk to the officer handling the case. Just then, the woman lunged at me with a kitchen knife that had been sitting on the counter. I saw her out of the corner of my eye just as the officer yelled to me. I turned, grabbed the woman's arm, and took her down to the floor. She didn't break. I didn't get hurt either, but she did go in full restraints, screaming to all the neighbors how we were trying to kill her.

9

WHAT'S A PIO?

I had five years on the department when I got an order to call PIO. Luckily, they gave me a phone number because I had no idea what PIO was. When the sergeant answered the phone, he said "Public Information Office." Oh, I thought to myself, that is the office that handles media calls, I think. The sergeant told me that he wanted me to come up to the office and talk to him about possibly working with them. My first thought was, Forget it; I don't even know what you do. I am having a great time right here on the street. I told him I would talk with them, and then I went to my supervisor and asked him what he thought. I was told that they don't make too many personal requests, and if I turned it down, they would probably never ask again. The experience would be good for me, and the street would always be there.

So I went up and talked with them. I was told they had looked over my reports and spoken to my supervisors and was told I was a very good writer and that I would do well on camera, so they would like me to join their team. I considered it carefully. I was very happy where I was and thought that I should stay but had been advised by a superior that I respected to take the position. So, now I had an inside job—still in uniform, but I met reporters instead of bad guys (depending on how you feel about reporters).

It was definitely different. I wrote news releases daily, updated the media on current events, and worked with detectives in major crimes on what information could be released. Part of my job was to respond to crime scenes, meet with the media, and explain what had happened. Imagine my surprise when the first case I was called out on was a fire at a multi-million dollar mansion with two fatalities, both children.

It was about one o'clock in the morning, and when I got to the home, I was greeted by hungry reporters looking for the story. I told them I would get back with them when I had some information. I went to the detectives on the scene for the story and was told that the children were still inside the home. They had been pronounced dead, and the mother was the only other person there. At that point, all we were releasing was the fact that we had received a 911 call from a woman who reported smoke coming from her neighbor's house. Upon the arrival of the fire department, two people had been found dead in the home and a third was still alive. This was all the information I could release for hours.

The reporters were as tired as I was and wanted more information, but investigations are not conducted in thirty minutes like they are on television. Family has to be notified, the crime scene needs to be scoured for evidence, and witnesses have to be interviewed and then reinterviewed. Every time someone went into or came out of the house, the cameras would light up in an attempt to capture every detail.

After about four hours, detectives brought the bodies of the children out. We hung up sheets because we didn't want the press to know the deceased were children yet and because they were partially burned so investigators did not want to put them in body bags, which might have destroyed some of the evidence. So the press filmed officers holding up sheets and then asked me what was going on. All I could tell them was that we had no further information to release at that time.

I was relieved by my Sergeant at about seven o'clock. I went home and got three hours of sleep before I had to be back at the office to field calls from media about the fatal fire. I turned on the television and saw my starched and well rested sergeant doing interviews with updates on the crime scene. I was the one there all night, and he does the interviews that they televise saying, "Officers had been on the scene all night trying to piece together the events of the night." He then goes on to say that two children had been found dead in the home, and the mother was being questioned by investigators.

I was later to find out that the somewhat unstable mother had put her two daughters to bed at about nine o'clock. About an hour later, she heard a lot of noise coming from the room, and when she went inside, she found the two girls, ages six and eight, making a tent out of the sheets and playing as if they were camping out. This outraged the mother, who then smothered both girls with pillows. She then tried to cover up the murders by setting the house on fire, only she had trouble doing that to such a big house, and the smoke was reported too soon. That was my indoctrination to PIO.

There were many cases such as these that I would report about during the next five years. It was a very interesting experience to work with the media. I did live television and radio shows, as well as crime reenactments. I would accompany detectives on drug and gambling raids in an effort to better report the cases to the press. It was not without some mishaps or faux pas, if you will.

Princess Diana from England was touring our area, and I was to accompany her entourage in case the press wanted some information. Because I knew I would be outside all day, I turned on the radio in my borrowed cruiser to catch a weather report. They said it was going to be very cold. I always wore a dress blouse for this duty, so I had to wear long underwear underneath. The next day, I met Princess Diana at her first stop and waited outside with the press. It was quite warm. Toasty, in fact. Almost hot. I couldn't understand why the weather report was so wrong. I was dying! I ran across the street to a Burger King and did a quick change in the restroom. I took off my entire uniform, ditched the long johns, and threw everything else back on. I took it back to my cruiser and put the air conditioner on for about two minutes, during which time I heard the station identifier for the radio station I had been listening to. It was in Cleveland, Ohio! The previous driver had somehow found this station and had the radio set to it.

Then there was the time I had call-out duty on Mother's Day. I had just been to church with my family and in-laws when I received a call to respond to a home nearby where a child had fallen into a backyard pool and drowned. Since I was already in a skirt suit, I responded to the scene as I was. When I saw myself on the news that night, I was not happy to see that I had neglected to remove my Mother's Day corsage when reporting the death of a child. That was kind of tacky.

℅

The crime reenactments were a part of the Crime Solvers program that I handled while assigned to PIO. Crime Solvers is an international program that offers cash for information that leads to an arrest and indictment of a suspect. These crimes are usually cold cases or very serious in nature. The reenactments were a lot of fun, and people enjoyed seeing that kind of report as opposed to just a talking head. I would also take anonymous phone tips and pass them on to the detectives. It was very gratifying when a tip led to a case closure. We had a civilian board of directors that would convene and vote on the amount of reward to give a caller based on the content of the call and where the information led. One of the board members or I would later meet the person at a place of his choosing and give him the money once he had given us his caller identification number. Some of those people looked very scary.

Of course, there were times you had to humor some callers who you knew didn't have any good information but just wanted you to think they did. I had a guy call me every Wednesday after my live television broadcast to talk about seedy people he knew and crimes he knew about. He was calling from prison. People in prison have a lot of good information, and you can't say you are not going to pay them just because they are in prison. So every Wednesday I would listen to this guy, and he would go on and on about things that had no value. He then started to write me letters, sometimes three in one day. The letters started to sound a little too personal and a little too freaky. I kept thinking this guy could get out one day and start stalking me, so I asked him one time when he was due to get out. I didn't want to ask him what he was in for because I thought that would be impolite. He never told me what he was in for, but he did tell me that he would never be out until he was a very old man. Comforting, I thought.

Often, we would rebroadcast unsolved crimes on the anniversary of the events in the hopes that it would stir someone's memory or attract some new information. It was often difficult when a loved one would call or come in to my office looking for help in solving a case that had gone on for some time. You want to do everything you can to help them, but there are times you can do nothing more. There are also some family members that give you more than they intended.

I was working late one night when a man came in my office asking for help in making some posters up to distribute about the homicide of his wife a few months earlier. I knew the husband was a suspect from the start and didn't want to say anything to him that a defense attorney would later call "inadmissible evidence," so I chose my words carefully and let him do the talking. The man went on to say how upset he was that his wife's murderer had not been found, and he wanted to do everything he could to help.

The murder took place in the parking lot of a busy shopping center just two weeks before Christmas. The woman's body was found in the passenger side of her car. The man was talking away about the case and said some things that only the killer would have known. He sent a shiver up my spine when he said, "Why don't you think anyone saw a family fight in that shopping center as busy as it was?" Family fight? Who said anything about a family fight? No one had reported anything about a family fight. The woman's body had been found in her car in the middle of the shopping center. I thought he was going to confess right there. I didn't want to question him even though he had come to me for help. So I placated him for awhile and then got rid of him. I picked up the phone and called the detective handling the case and told him what had happened. The guy never did confess to killing his wife, and the case is still unsolved, but everyone knew who really did it; they just couldn't prove it. It was chilling to sit there in front of a man I knew killed his wife and just play along as if he was the victim.

I never heard from him again; however, I saw him on the news on the first anniversary of his wife's death. He had grown a beard and moustache and was sitting next to his new wife. It was very strange to think he had moved on so quickly and changed his appearance so drastically. It begs the question, "Who are you, and what are you concealing behind your new appearance?"

10

HUMOR ... IT *IS* THE BEST MEDICINE

When you are a rookie, if other cops like you, they will play jokes on you, like have you set up an LZ (landing zone) for a helicopter landing only for no helicopter to arrive. They will also send you on fictitious calls or give you a lookout for an old white-haired man dressed in red and white with black boots. (That call comes around every Christmas.) On one evening, I was dispatched to a cul-de-sac for a "suspicious vehicle." The "caller" said the car had been sitting in the middle of the road and was running with no apparent driver. When I got to the location, I was only too surprised to find my car sitting there. Seems the boys had gotten hold of my keys in the locker room, driven it to my patrol area, and left it.

Fortunately, there is a great deal of humor in police work. You can either laugh and have a good time, or let it eat at you and die young. It all depends on your attitude.

As I have said before, the midnight shift can be very long, and we have to entertain ourselves and each other from time to time. Joe was from New York. He came down to Virginia to get a job in police work because we were hiring, and New York wasn't. The average life expectancy of a native New Yorker in Virginia was about two years, and then they would almost always go home. Joe was no different, but while he was with us, he was a riot. It was about four o'clock on a very rainy morning when I was walking up to the station from my cruiser to do a little paperwork. Joe drove into the lot at mach nine as they do in New York. He was wearing a shower cap, sporting sunglasses with the eyeballs that pop out on springs, and singing, "She's got Bette Davis eyes!" I laughed until my sides hurt.

A couple of nights later, Joe came into the station and said, "Lieutenant, are you in a good mood?"

My reply was, "I was, Joe. Are you going to mess that up for me?"

"Well," Joe said. "I got to talking with someone out at the gas pumps, and I kind of drove off with the pump still in my car." With that, Joe handed me the half of the gas pump that had been left in his tank. It's really hard to write someone up for destroying property when they make you laugh while they confess.

One time I went into another district to investigate a hit-and-run. I had no idea where I was. It was dark, and as I rounded a curve, I saw a nude man standing on the corner. As I went by, I saw a car coming toward me with a woman and several small children inside. Needless to say, I was a little flustered and was trying to read street signs to advise the dispatcher of my location. After describing the events to her, she asked me if the exposure was a felony or misdemeanor. (A felony exposure is one that is witnessed by a child under the age of thirteen. All other exposures are misdemeanors.) My reply was, "I am not sure; I will have to go back and check." The guys went nuts. My computer screen lit up with comments like, "Hey, Connie. It's not the size of the penis that makes it a felony or misdemeanor." What my fellow officers didn't know was that I was trying to find out if the vehicle I had seen with the children had witnessed the incident. By the time I got turned around, the guy, the car, and my self-respect were gone for the evening.

 confidence

Christmas is a hard time to work if you have a family. When I was a sergeant, I asked my lieutenant if I could cook the guys Christmas breakfast in the station during the midnight shift. Christmas Eve was usually a slow night, and my lieutenant agreed to cover the street if something were to happen. I had a very elaborate setup. I was dressed like one of Santa's elves and had several electric frying pans set up on the roll call room table. I planned scrambled eggs, sausage, and hash browns. At about one o'clock in the morning, I started to cook. Everything was going fine until the third electric frying pan was plugged in, and the station lights went out. Oops! Power overload, I guessed. Well, it seemed easy enough to find the circuit box with a flashlight, flip the breaker, and move on. But it continued to happen two more times. I consolidated the eggs and sausage and unplugged one of the frying pans much to the delight of my lieutenant.

I got ready to call in the first two officers when the floodgates opened up. For some reason, the bad guys weren't cooperating, and it turned out to be the busiest Christmas Eve on record. What was I to do with all this food? I knocked out power to the whole station three times for this? I decided the troops would eat well one way or another. I took two plates out at a time and stood outside the station near the main road. The station was in the center of the district and just about everyone would have to pass by this area at some point. My Christmas breakfast plans would not be ruined! I had my lieutenant tell all the guys to come by the station on the way to their next call. I handed out breakfast platters, and they quickly scurried off. The station had become a Christmas breakfast drive-through.

ⁿ

Bars are great places to go and watch people make fools of themselves. And you don't have to be in uniform to do that. One of the bars on my beat alternated hard rock, country, and easy listening to please everyone. The hard rock nights were the best for watching idiots. The girls would wear torn stockings with very short skirts and heavy, dark makeup, and the guys would say, "wow" and "dude" a lot. A couple of us would line up outside and watch the parade and then go inside and make sure everyone was behaving themselves. After so many arrests for drugs and bar fights, the county would take away the bar's liquor license, and they would be out of business, so the owners weren't always happy to see us. One young lady walked by me and looked me over like I was from another planet, yet she was wearing a torn shirt, torn skirt with matching stockings, and green hair. After she passed, one of my fellow officers said, "Where do you buy stuff like that?" Without hesitation, another officer replied, "Sluts-R-Us."

෴

A lot of bars have dartboards, and I arrived at a bar shortly after a fight was called. No officer was hurt, and we got the bad guys, but we all had to laugh when one officer came out with four darts sticking out of his bulletproof vest. He didn't know they were there, and the vest had certainly come in handy that night.

෴

I am prone to getting sun poisoning on my lips when I am out in the sun too long. At one such time, my husband developed a black eye when his face came into contact with my brother-in-law's knee during a friendly family game of full-contact whiffle ball. It just so happened that my husband and I were both on the same supervisory committee representing two different stations and had to be at a meeting in the chief's office at the same time. Ron walked in first and was heckled by several of the other supervisors sitting at the table. When I arrived, the jokes were on as far as "who had won the fight." When the chief arrived at the meeting, he looked around the room, saw both of our injuries, sat down, smiled, and said, "I don't want to know."

The laughter never stopped right up to the day I retired. I would often bring a banana and yogurt to work, but sometimes the banana would sit on my desk all day before I got the chance to eat it. Several times I would come in off the road and the words "eat me" were written on my banana. I had two suspects. Both were known pranksters, and both had filled my locker and office with toilet paper the day after I announced my retirement. On my final day, I returned to the station, and there sat my banana. In large dark letters were the words, "Eat me. We will all miss you."

11

A Façade of Stone

Often people dehumanize police officers. We get stared at all the time whether we're in our cruisers, in a store, or in a restaurant. I was eating alone in a fast food restaurant one night, and I heard a little boy who was about five say to his mother, "Look, that cop over there is eating." That was the last time I ate alone in a restaurant.

It is difficult to understand what cops are all about unless you are one or you are married to one. I was both. I married a cop I met on the job, and we were married for twenty years before we divorced. That, in itself, is a miracle. Most police officers marry at least twice; it's not an easy profession to understand. The hours are long, the work is stressful, and often it isn't easy to share this with another person who isn't in the same profession.

Nothing is closer than the "family" of cops. We share each others' problems. We go to each others' picnics, weddings, and funerals. When a cop needs something, his "family" is there. When a cop has to stay after work to unwind with the guys, it's understood. It's not a job you leave at the office, because you are always thinking about it. A case may haunt you. An event may disturb you. You may even second guess something you did that day. The job can leave you feeling very much alone. This may be one reason the suicide rate for cops is high and why many bail out before retirement.

Cops have coping strategies much like others who work in professions that are emotionally and mentally draining. We make jokes to separate ourselves from the reality of a difficult situation. It's effective and healthy, because it allows you to take a step back and have some perspective. We can't fix the world, and we can't take all problems in our hearts. We have to move on.

A lot of people don't see it that way, though. They expect us to go into a fight, bust it up, take away the bad guys, and fifteen minutes later have compassion for a poor misguided youth who just robbed a convenience store "because he comes from a broken home." We are expected to be preachers, doctors, lawyers, marriage counselors, psychologists, teachers, parents, mentors, sharpshooters, and auto mechanics all rolled up into one. Many times I've walked in on scenes where everyone was yelling and screaming and running around, and I had to assess the situation within seconds and take action. These opposing expectations create a great deal of pressure for a police officer.

Sometimes you don't have the luxury of assessment; you just have to act. I was called to a shopping center where two people were arguing. When I pulled up, the girl ran off, and the man shouted, "She is trying to kill herself!" I took off running after the girl, who chose to run across a busy road and into the woods. When I caught up with her, I tackled her and grabbed her by the wrists to control her. Imagine my surprise when I realized that she had cut both wrists and was bleeding everywhere.

Thirty minutes later I was at the scene of a horrific car accident where I watched a sixteen-year-old boy die in the arms of a paramedic when rescuers lifted a gravel truck off his convertible. I wish that people would understand more about what really goes on in the life of a police officer rather than what they see on television.

One warm Sunday morning, I was called to the scene of a suicide in a new neighborhood where only one tree remained after the bulldozers had cleared the way for houses. A sixteen-year-old boy had hanged himself in that tree the night before. Dad had discovered him when he got up the next morning and cut him down. What I later learned was that Dad had also zipped up his sons pants when he found him. It seemed that the suicide was actually an accidental death. The boy had several sexually explicit magazines in his bedroom. One such magazine taught him that if he attempted to temporarily cut off his airway when masturbating that the feeling would become more intense. The boy had been trying this out but had made the rope too strong and could not regain control after his orgasm. Dad was too embarrassed to tell us. The boy had been a genius, able to build anything. He had made a radio into a radio/flashlight combination so he could see his way into the woods at night. His Dad had seen him go into the woods the night before, even carrying a rope, but he never questioned it.

I went to several accidental deaths and suicides in my career. I had never even heard of some of the things people do to themselves and others before I became a cop. I do think I could have lived a very happy life without ever knowing some of these things.

I have been to every type of death call there is, from "jumpers" (people who jump off buildings to commit suicide) to overdoses to terminally ill individuals, and I never got used to them. We would always have to check over a body to make sure it didn't have any bullet holes or stab wounds that were not obvious before we called the medical examiner or funeral home. I hated doing that; I just can't stand to touch a dead body.

My first death case was while I was in training. My field training officer and I were called to a house where no one had seen the woman in two weeks, and her mail and newspapers had been piling up—it was in July. We couldn't get into the house without forcing a window, so my training officer went in first. As soon as the window was cracked, we knew what was inside. The smell was something I'll never forget. The other officer told me he would unlock the front door for me but to "watch out for the maggots." I laughed and said, "Yeah, right." But when I stepped in, the maggots were racing for the door. Seems they like fresh air too. When rescue came to take her away, they had trouble getting the body bag all the way into the ambulance because of some equipment that was in the way, so they slammed the door shut. That was just enough pressure to let the build-up of gases in the woman's body explode within the bag. It made a popping sound and would not have been pretty when the bag was opened in the medical examiner's office. I got out of there fast, went home after the shift, took a shower, and threw all my clothes in the wash. What a great introduction to death investigation.

Then there was the boy who went over to his girlfriend's house to help her move. There was a note on the door saying how sorry she was, but too many things had gone wrong, etc.

The boyfriend didn't even want to go in by himself, so he called us. The major problem with these kinds of cases is we have no idea what we are going to find. Will there really be a dead person? If so, in what form, and where will that person be? Will the person be armed hoping for "death by cop"? On this particular case, I got a call from an officer who was new with our department but had come from another, and he wanted to know if he could come to this scene because he had never been on a suicide. "Great," I said, "you can help find the body." He came over and three of us methodically and slowly searched the house, which had been boxed up like she was moving away. The young lady was found hanging by the water pipe in the basement. I thought the new officer was going to lose it, but he hung in there. He did get pale when the crime scene technicians responded and needed his help to cut her down and carefully lay her on the floor. He never asked to come to another death scene.

The most unbelievable death case I ever went on was the case of "the girl with the purple hair." The call came in as a "malicious wounding in progress." I was pretty far away and wasn't sure of the area I was going to. More information was coming into the communications center from a man. He was saying that his twenty-five-year-old daughter had stabbed his wife and was trying to kill him. Several units were responding, as well as the helicopter. I was doing as much as I could from ten miles out, and I didn't want to have one of my officers go in until I got there. Communications kept the man on the phone who said his daughter had left to go walk the dog. Okay, perfectly understandable—kill your parents and then go walk the dog. The man also said that the suspect had purple hair. I kept making wrong turns trying to get there until the helicopter sort of guided me in.

I had several officers looking for the suspect and going door to door when I arrived.

The woman was dead, and the man who had been on the phone was being treated by rescue. He had been stabbed multiple times but was quite coherent. Too coherent I thought at first. He was so talkative that I thought he had made up the whole thing. He told me that his daughter came into the bedroom while he and his wife were watching TV and stabbed her mother to death—about thirty-six times. She then came after the father, who locked himself in the bathroom. Every time the father would attempt to exit the bathroom, the daughter would stick the knife in the opening and slash at him again. He almost bled to death in the bathroom, which was evident by the amount of coagulated blood in there. One officer who went into the bedroom before me almost knocked me down the stairs trying to get outside before he threw up.

The father waited in the bathroom for several minutes before deciding to make a run for the closet where he had a shotgun stashed. He threw open the door, ran for the closet, and loaded the shotgun. He checked on his wife and then watched as his daughter casually left the house walking their dog. When I asked him if she had a car, he said no. He was laughing as he told the story and invited me in to the ambulance to "join him." I sent an officer to the hospital to stay with him and then continued the investigation. One of the neighbors said that the girl did have purple hair, and she did have a car, which was missing. I started to believe the man now. As it turned out, the reason he acted the way he did was because he was in shock. He didn't fully grasp what had happened and wasn't able to discuss details for four days. The daughter was stopped by a Pennsylvania State Trooper who was at the end of his shift when he spotted her car on the side of the road. Thinking that the woman was disabled, the trooper approached the car and asked her what the problem was. The woman, covered in blood, responded with, "I just killed my parents."

I think if anyone were to ask any police officer what the most difficult case was of their career, they would recall one involving a child. We've all had them. Children are the most precious examples of innocence that God ever created, and when that innocence is bruised, my gloves come off. I supervised the Child Services Unit for a time and could never have worked those cases for very long. The public never hears about crimes against children unless it is a highly publicized case involving death. Often the psychological scars are far worse than the physical scars, but these don't make the headlines. It never ceased to amaze me the things people would do to their children in the name of discipline.

My husband had a case involving a missing autistic boy who had run away from his caregiver. It was getting dark and cold, and the boy needed to be found. After hours of searching, my husband found the boy—or at least part of him; he had been hit by a train. He told me about it later that night, and he kept clearing his throat as he spoke. I know the sight of the boy is probably etched in his memory forever. I know he held our son a little closer that night.

I, too, had a case involving a child that will forever haunt me. I went to the home of a family who had delivered their first child at home prematurely. The mother was in distress, and the father helped deliver the infant before paramedics could arrive. When I got there, the baby had already been transferred to the hospital. The parents had been notified that the baby was stillborn.

Police are often called to homes if a death occurs and the patient is not under a doctor's care. The officer had taken the basic information, and the mother and father were also being transported to the hospital so that the mother could be checked out. When I got to the hospital, I told a nurse that I needed to examine the baby, which is procedure in death cases. The nurse told me that they were very busy that night and that there were no empty rooms to put the baby in, so they "put it in there." With that, she pointed to a closed door.

Thinking it was a small examination room, I opened the door and was horrified to find that the baby, wrapped in a blanket, was on a shelf in the broom closet. The two investigators and I could barely fit in to shut the door behind us. I had to move one of the trash cans and a mop out in the hall. After we examined the baby for any signs of foul play, I went back out into the hall to catch my breath. I was told that the mother wanted to hold the baby one more time. I was once again horrified to find that the mother was in the room directly across the hall from the closet that held her baby—if she had known what I knew. I immediately grabbed a head nurse and told her of the situation and that she was to take the baby out of the closet and find a room so that this mother could have a final and dignified farewell with her baby. The nurse did as I requested.

In this profession, we can't cry, we can't show emotion. But I couldn't eat. I couldn't function. I couldn't stop thinking about that baby and the further pain the mother would have endured had she known what had transpired. That night, as I lay in bed looking up at the ceiling, thinking of the unimaginable pain that the parents must have been going through and thinking of how lucky I was to have had two healthy and beautiful children, I heard crying. As I strained to make out where it was coming from, I realized it was me.

12

WHEN THE FAT LADY SINGS

A couple of years after I was hired, they changed the retirement from twenty to twenty-five years of required service. However, I was grandfathered in and could therefore retire with full benefits after twenty years. When I had less than ten years on, twenty years seemed like forever, but that nineteenth year crept up quickly, and before I knew it, I started thinking about the next twenty years. I tended to take on a different attitude. I started getting a little lax. I didn't wear my vest as often; I took chances. I started telling people what I really thought. I had dealt with a certain element for so long that I couldn't help but get a little cynical. I'd heard the same excuses and complaints so many times that I could finish people's sentences for them, but I couldn't really tell them what I thought unless I wanted to spend the last few months of my career in internal affairs.

I started to take note of the "little voices" that seemed to be directing me toward retirement. Of course, the loudest voices came from my kids. I was putting my daughter to bed one night, and she asked if we were going to spend the whole day together the next day. What she meant was would she be seeing me for a couple of hours before work or would I have the whole day off to be with her.

My kids were forced to grow up with two cops as parents. My son knew all the rules of the road by age six. One day I heard him tell his nanny, "You better leave me alone, or my mom and dad will take you to jail." I have a lithograph called "Priorities," which says, "A hundred years from now it will not matter what my bank account was, the sort of house I lived in, or the kind of car I drove … but the world may be different because I was important in the life of a child."

Statistically, retired cops don't live very long after retirement. To me, that is very sad. I keep thinking that some officers retire with no other interests and never take care of themselves. When you think about retiring, you have to find something that gives you that tingle back, that excitement you had when you were first recruited or when you first start dating someone new. For me, it was my kids. When they heard me talking about retiring, they started telling people, "My mommy might come and work in my school." I retired for them. They needed me more than I needed the job. They were six and ten, and I felt a real need to focus on them.

Don't get me wrong. It didn't make it easy to retire. It just made it more practical and sensible. I didn't have to look around for another job for very long. Actually, I had several offers to choose from, but when a position opened up in a school for a safety specialist with law enforcement background, it was a no-brainer. I jumped on it.

Weekends, holidays, snow days, and the summer off with my kids. What could be more perfect? Still, when I announced my retirement, it came as a great surprise to most people. My commander refused to accept my letter of retirement stating,

"You can't go! You're one of my best." Hearing that put a lump in my throat the size of Texas. It didn't get any easier from there. I couldn't put my heart and soul into something for twenty years and just walk out the door. Many officers sent me messages and made comments that I will hold dear for the rest of my life. I will always remember the ones who believed in me and supported me throughout my career. Of course, my family was always my best support. My husband understood that I worked with almost all men, so most of my friends would be men. He understood when I stayed after work some nights to share war stories with the guys, and he stood by me in the bad times when pressures became intense. Not too many husbands could do that.

But there were others who were always there when I needed them. At times I felt that I had a hundred big brothers. If I found myself in a physical confrontation or a traffic stop, I would look back, and there would always be someone there, looking out for me. To those officers, I say, "Thank you," with a big hug. To the other officers who felt that women belonged in the kitchen, I say, "Get over it. You need us, and we are here to stay."

I chose to clean out my locker and desk when the fewest number of people were around. I had always surrounded myself with pictures of my kids and my husband, but then there were those other things tucked away in the back that had told my story. A card sent to me on Thanksgiving from a six-year-old girl who had been missing for about ten hours one freezing winter night. Pictures of criminals who I had successfully prosecuted. Case files and notes about crimes that had some meaning for me over the years. Notes from superiors congratulating me on a job well done. Photographs of my locker after a fellow officer decorated it and stuffed my shoes and uniform with toilet paper. A banana that said "Eat me" on it. Pictures of my surprise fortieth birthday party. How do you choose between the job you love and the family you love? You look at those innocent faces that count on you, and you know the right decision to make.

Then the day came—the last day on the job. Everything I did routinely was now being done for the last time. I put on the uniform—for the last time. I shined my shoes and brass—for the last time. I held roll call—for the last time. I patrolled the streets—for the last time. I made decisions that would affect the lives of other people—for the last time. As I pulled up to the station parking lot, an officer came out and said, "Aren't you going to say something when you sign off today?" I hadn't even thought about it. What do you say for the last time? I told him I couldn't, but at the urging of many, I picked up the mic—for the last time. I told the dispatcher, "Car 4 Baker, sign me off at the station—for the last time, God bless you." With that, the tears welled up inside me, and officers poured out of the station with smiles and hugs that I will never forget. One young officer said, "Thank you for all you've done. You made a difference." And isn't that what we are really on this earth to do?

It's been a few years now since I retired, and it's really just settling in that I have left a career I truly loved for a family I love even more. But I've moved on. It's over. I'm okay. I made a difference.

Even with all the changes over the years, few women seek the profession of law enforcement, and fewer still stay until retirement. The reasons are vast. The job is very physically and emotionally draining. Raising children is difficult because of the long and fluctuating hours. It can be dangerous and is very demanding. The police department expects its officers to be fully devoted to the department. Officers count on each other to be there for them as backup officers, to trade working days, or to cover for them when they need leave.

When I was hired in 1979, there were only about seven hundred sworn officers of whom only about thirty were women, and only one was a supervisor. I was the eighth woman to ever retire from the Fairfax County Police Department and am proud to have known all the professional men and women that comprise that law enforcement agency.

After retirement, I spent five years in school security, which provided a great schedule for my kids, but I was bored to death. I was encouraged to apply for another law enforcement job. Today, I am chief of police in Warrenton, Virginia. My children are proud of me, and my daughter rode beside me in the grand marshal's car in the July 4 parade. I am back doing what I love to do and still making a difference.